FOR VICTORY
Collectibles

Martin S. Jacobs

Pictorial Histories Publishing Company, Inc.
Missoula, Montana

COPYRIGHT © 2001 MARTIN S. JACOBS
All rights reserved. No part of this book may be used or
reproduced without written permission of the author.

LIBRARY OF CONGRESS CONTROL # 2001 135251

ISBN # 1-57510-089-4

First Printing October 2001
Printed in Canada by
Hignell Book Printing
Winnipeg, Manitoba

Front Cover: Milk Bottle ($150-225), Comic Book ($175-225), Sterling Jeweled Pin ($200-225), Poster ($175-225), License Plate Topper ($75-100), Glass Picture Frame ($35-45)
Back Cover: Ceramic Coin Bank ($125-150), Comb Display ($100-125), Carry-all Cart ($125-150), Sailor and Nurse Statue ($1,000-1,500), Ceramic Vase ($150-175), "V" Pins Display ($125-150)

Layout by: Anna McBrayer
Typography by: Anna McBrayer
Cover and color page design by: Mike Egeler
on Machintosh utilizing
Adobe Photoshop 5.5
QuarkXPress 4.0

PICTORIAL HISTORIES PUBLISHING COMPANY, INC.
713 South Third West, Missoula, Montana 59801
Phone: (406) 549-8488   FAX: (406) 728-9280   phpc@montana.com

Introduction

Where it started, no one really knows. Suddenly the "V" sign was all over Europe in 1941. In the conquered countries, people chalked it on walls, cut it out of paper and drew it in the dust on automobiles. In an effort to undermine the Axis' morale, the people of all the subjugated nations heeded the urging of our allies in using the "V" sign by waving two fingers in a "V" shape as they passed on the street.

As far away as Naples, Italy, it was not uncommon to see an abandoned bomb shelter off the road with a hand-painted "V" on a concrete wall. Almost overnight, it became the simple, universal symbol of resistance to German occupation.

In most languages in Europe, "V" meant Victory. To the French, it stood for Victoire, to the Dutch - Vryjheid (freedom), to the Czechs - Vitezstvi (victory), to the Serbs - Vitestvo (freedom), with the Norwegians embracing the English "Victory."

The "V" symbol had doubly good fortune as it was audible as well as visual. In the Morse code, "V" was three dots and a dash. Clerks rapped it out with pencils, drummers beat it on drums, restaurant diners tapped it on glasses to summon a waiter and motorists tooted it on their horns.

Springing up spontaneously on the continent, the "V" was quickly spread by the work of a talented broadcaster on the British Broadcasting Company. Calling himself "Colonel Britton," he called attention to the dit-dit-dit-dah rhythm as forming the opening notes to Beethoven's Fifth Symphony. Never deciphered by the Germans, the (...-) was later incorporated with the sign for Victory.

Although battles were taking place far away from U.S. boarders- on Pacific Islands, Europe and in North Africa- the war was never far from everyone's mind back home. After the attack on Pearl Harbor, Americans in the United States got into the act and staged wild recruiting rallies, cheering our departing GI's, singing patriot songs and dancing to the "Victory Polka." As patriotism grew to a fevered pitch, the "V for Victory" sign was plastered everywhere. It soon became an icon for victory in support of our troops. In windows of nearly every patriotic American home, a banner read: "This is a Victory Home." Inside, a "V-Home Certificate" was usually displayed in a prominent place. Large-sized, inexpensive posters with colorfully touted themes of recruitment, food conservation, danger of espionage, and war bonds, exemplified the "V for Victory" symbol which became synonymous with the war effort.

In the midst of the war, more than two-million babies were born. Labeled as "Victory babies," it was not uncommon to see the "V" emblazoned on baby carriages, as well as on baby diapers. Having grown fashionable, patriotism was demonstrated by Americans of all ages by displaying "V for Victory" pins and buttons on their uniforms, hats, coats and dresses.

During the war, farmers were busy growing food for our troops, but food was in short supply on the home front. The Secretary of Agriculture encouraged Americans to grow fresh vegetables by purchasing "Victory Seeds" and planting "Victory Gardens." In Tennessee, farmers that grew their own food received "V - certificates" (Vitamins for Victory) from the government. The Automobile Club of America distributed "V" auto tags that clipped onto a license plate and a windshield sticker that read: "Drive for Victory." At the request of the Treasury Department, Walt Disney Studios designed and incorporated the "V" into its emblems, patches and decals which helped promote the sale of war savings bonds. Even funny paper characters of the day got involved in the war effort. Joe Palooka joined the army and wrote a "V" patch proliferating the "V for Victory"

Today, the "V for Victory" sign routinely shows up at flea markets, paper shows and on the internet. Embellished with the artwork of the 1940's, it's almost always found in the traditional red, white and blue. Once the image catches our collector's eyes, we begin to see it everywhere. For it is the fervor generated by a single letter of the alphabet, this history of our world during WWII that makes those items that carry the "V" sign so highly collectible today.

There will be millions of words written about World War II, but there will be one shinning, indelible memory which will never be forgotten but will be shared forever by our sailors, soldiers, airmen, medics, marines and those patriotic Americans who contributed to winning the war - the "V for Victory" icon!

Foreword

After the attack on Pearl Harbor on December 7, 1941, Franklin Delano Roosevelt told the nation, "We are going to win the war, and we are going to win the peace that follows."

Upon America's entrance into World War II, it was clear to Americans that industry needed all the manpower, materials and facilities to increase war production to whatever levels that were required for "Victory." Success was due to the will of Americans to do the jobs that were imposed by total war efforts to produce weapons, artillery, airplanes, food and supplies for our troops. The war was a clear call for everyone's contribution and cooperation--including our children, young adults, men and women--to work together in one common cause, as well as in determination for "Victory."

Jean Milgram "Victory Girl"

In mid-1943, with the United States fully involved in the war, 21-year-old Jean Milgram pitched into the war effort and went to work in the commissary at Fort Blanding Army Base in Key West, Florida. For $25 a week, her help in assisting GIs with cigarettes and candy went far beyond her call of duty. Jean regularly reached out with her great smile and her "magnetic" personality to thousands of soldiers during their most emotionally vulnerable periods before departing to foreign soils. Around Camp Blanding, Jean was quickly referred to as everyone's "Victory Girl." She provided our boys with much needed friendship. To most of them, Jean was a fond reminder of the sweetheart they left behind. Jean recalls that her fondest memories from the war years were of all of the young men and women she met who gladly served their country with no self-pity and no malice.

Today, Jean is 81-years-old and is in excellent health. "I still wear my favorite 'V for Victory' pins to my volunteer jobs, the same ones I wore at the PX over 58 years ago," she says.

The same dedication surely can be attributed to the thousands of selfless workers like Jean Milgram, who were an inspiration to our country to win the war!

On May 20, 2001, Martin Jacobs and Jean Milgram visited the Victory Store at the entrance to the USS Missouri Battleship Memorial at Pearl Harbor, Hawaii.

Table of Contents

Introduction	iii
Foreword	iv
Pearl Harbor	v
Banks	1
Music	4
V-mail	6
Postcards	8
Postal Covers	11
Stamps and Bonds	15
Linens	18
Banners	20
Greeting Cards	22
Victory Gardens	25
Sports	28
Movies	30
Books, Booklets, Magazines and Comics	32
Products	38
Jewelry, Buttons, Patches and Ribbons	41
Cindarellas, Stickers and Decals	47
Posters	52
Toys and Playthings	57
Advertisements	66
Miscellaneous	71
Chronology of Significant World War Two Victories	85
Victory Celebrations	86
September 2, 1945	87
About the Author	88
Contributors	88

About the Pricing: The estimated price values that I have listed in this book are not intended to be a definite guide to the price one will or should pay for the "V for Victory" collectibles. I understand how important it is to quote the most accurate value possible, however, values are not cast in stone, they are fluid. An item's value is what someone is willing to pay for it. Understand that values change by every auction and every sale. Therefore, these prices are intended to keep in perspective the prices of various items and thereby to assist one who decides to build a collection. Also, prices in this guide assume that the item is complete as when it was new and in very good condition.

OPENING NOTES, BEETHOVEN'S SYMPHONY NO. V

Pearl Harbor

REMEMBER PEARL HARBOR- When America plunged into war in 1941, the phrase "Remember Pearl Harbor" soon emerged, not only to memorialize the events of that historic day but also to serve as a timeless call for collective vigilance and unity. Together, with the "V for Victory" symbol, the phrase entered American folklore instantly, and its popularity soon dictated its appearance on a variety of items such as posters, patches, license plate toppers, matchbooks and other related wartime products.

Celluloid Button ($25-35)
Silk Banner ($75-85)

Paper Cup ($20-25)
Match Cover ($7-10)
Postal Cover ($15-20)

Metal License Plate ($75-100)

Banks

The need for more production inspired children to save their allowances to buy savings bonds. Most banks were constructed of "nonessential" materials such as wood, plastic and chalkware. Though "V for Victory" was immortalized on every bank imaginable, these banks were a welcome addition to every household. Leading suppliers of banks were American Toy Works, Louis Marks and Co., Wolverine and FAO Swartz Co.

Pressboard ($125-150)

Cardboard and Wood ($175-225)

Plaster ($85-100)

Chalkware ($100-125)

Cardboard ($85-100)

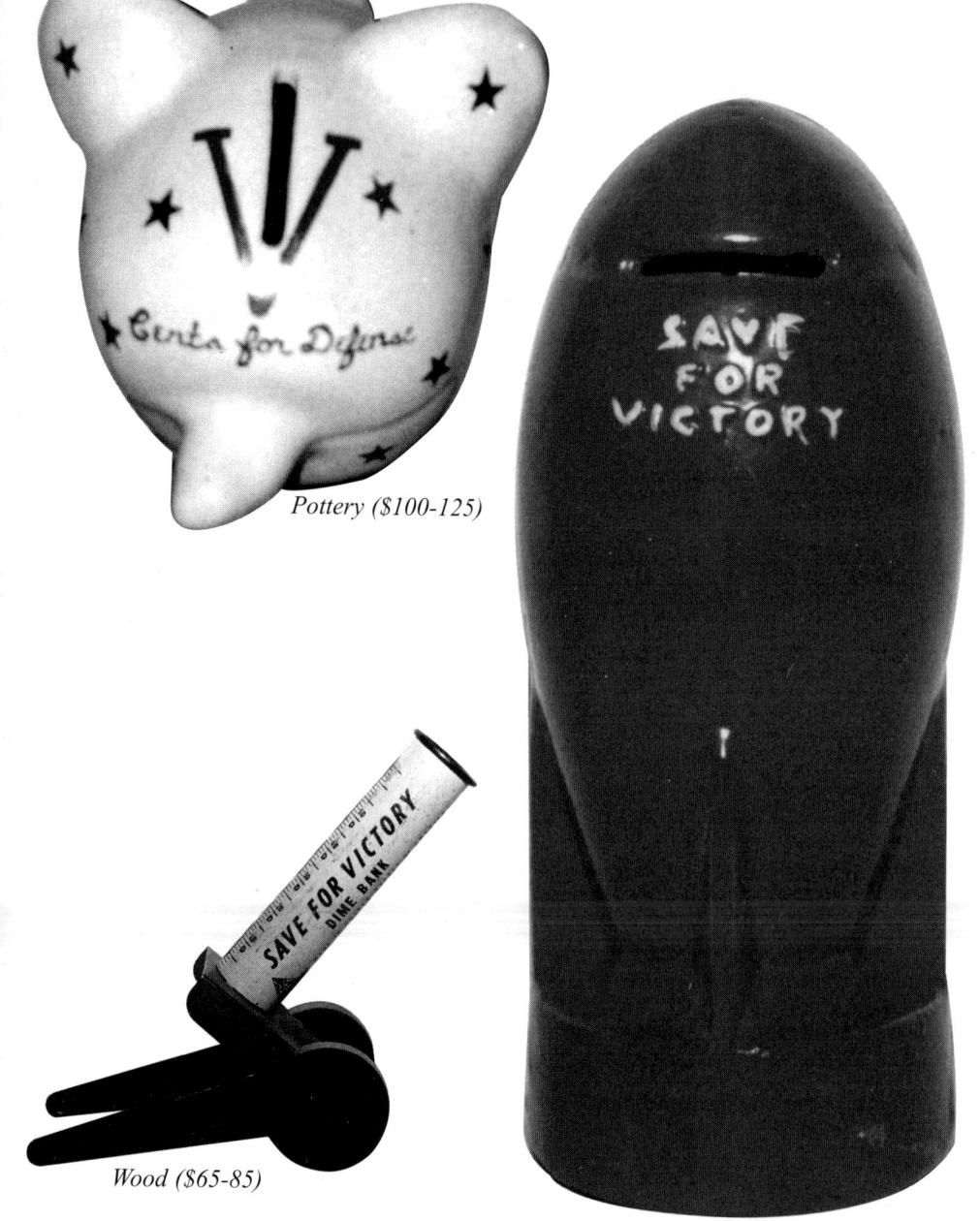

"V for Victory" Collectibles

Pottery ($100-125)

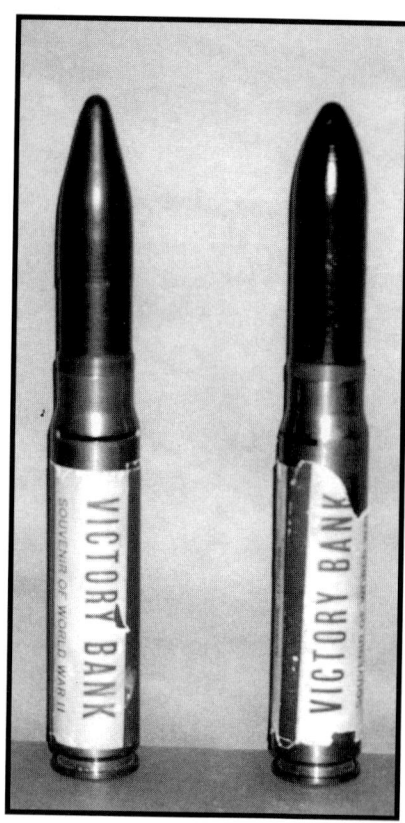

20mm Shells ($75-100)

Wood ($65-85)

Wood Composition ($65-85)

Plaster ($85-100)

Ceramic ($50-75), ($25-50)

Banks

Tin ($65-85)

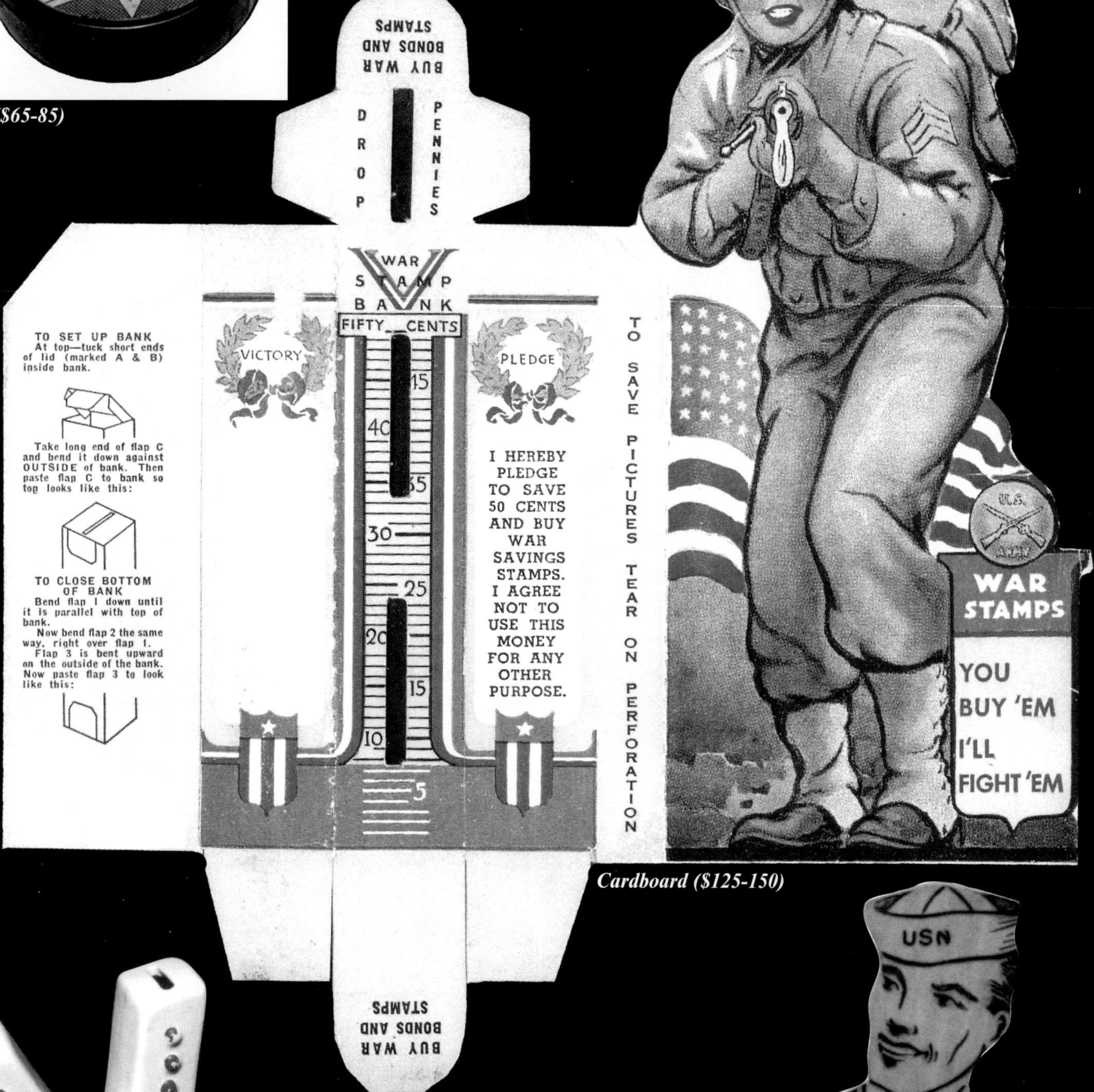

Cardboard ($125-150)

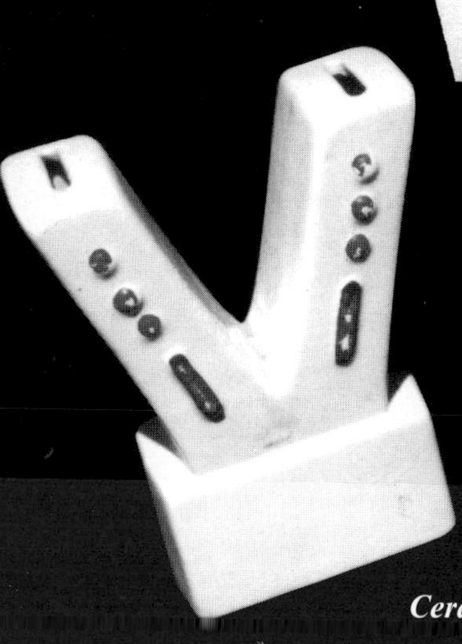

Ceramic ($100-125)   *Wood ($125-150)*

Music

America's best known musicians and songwriters released dozens of song sheets featuring strong cover graphics while proliferating "V for Victory," and performed by the popular personalities of the era, including Bing Crosby, Sammy Kaye, Frank Sinatra and others. Standard Music Size 9"x12".
Assorted Song Sheets ($15-20)

"V for Victory" Collectibles

Assorted Song Sheets ($15-20)

V-Mail

Ink Bottle ($25-35)

Stationary ($35-45)

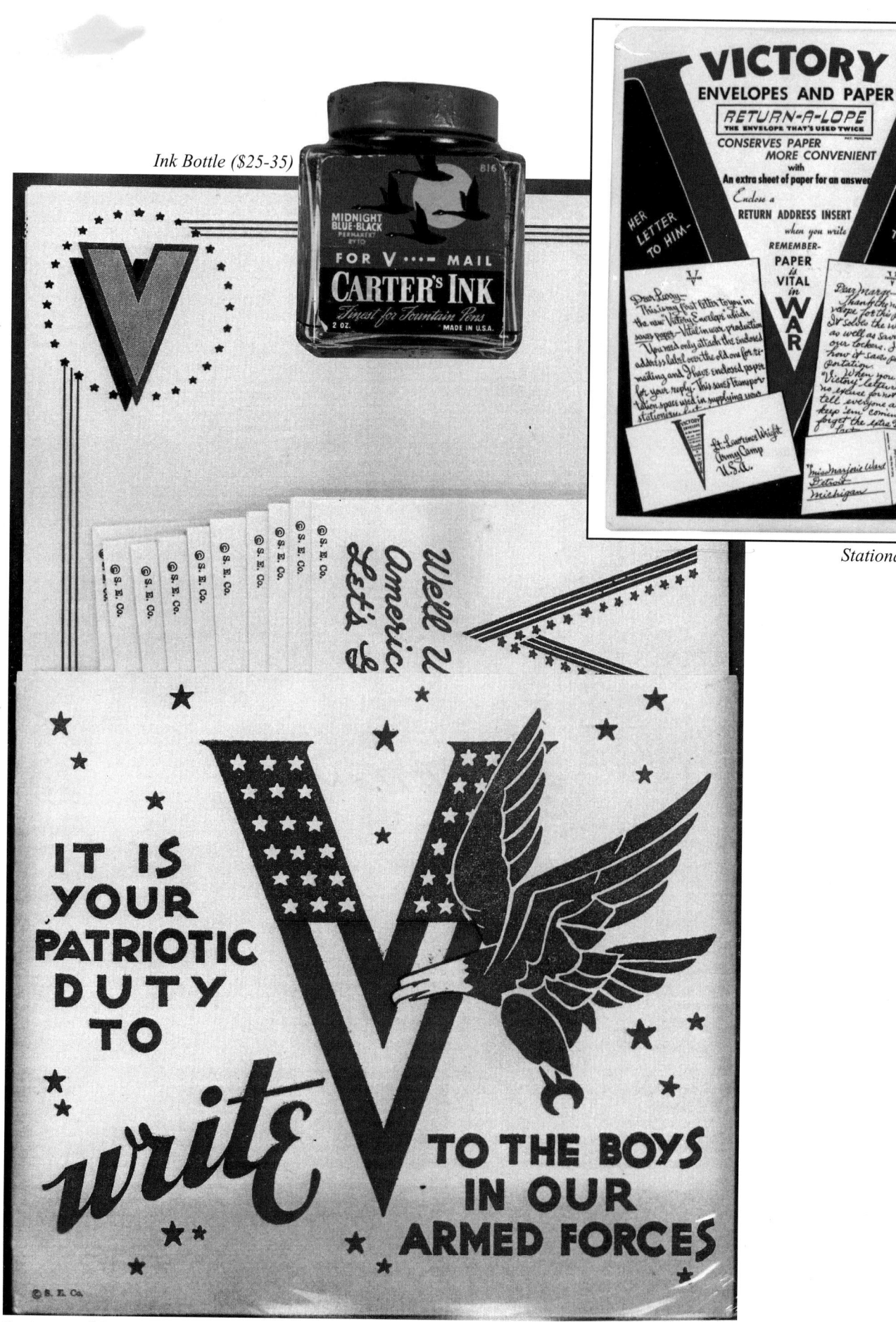

Stationary ($35-45)

"V for Victory" Collectibles

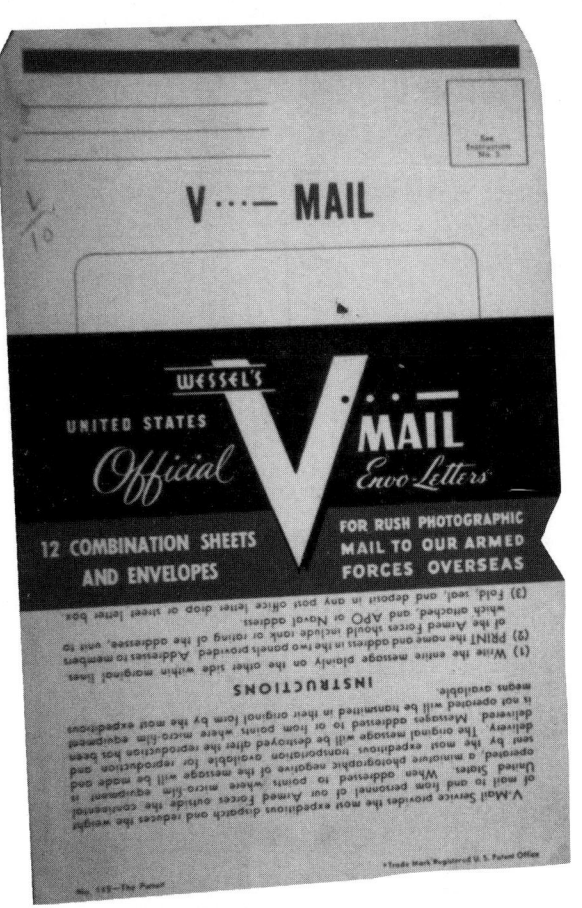

V-Mail Packet ($20-25)

Ink Bottle ($25-35)

Pencil Lead ($15-20)

Cardboard Container ($45-55)

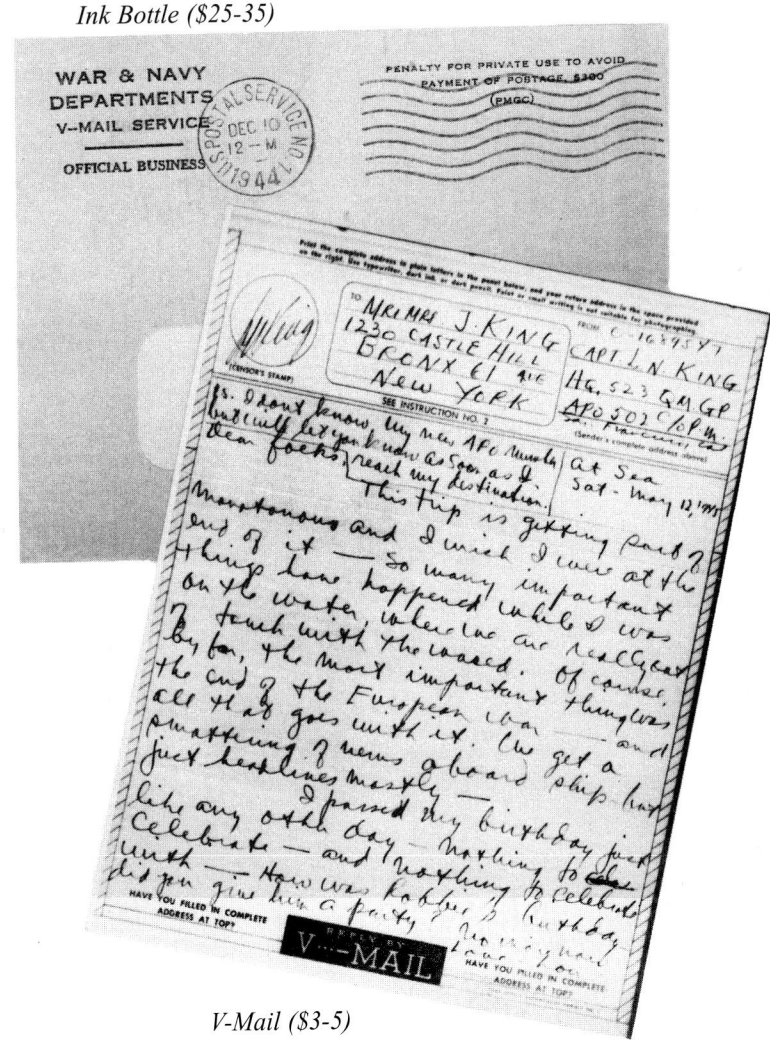

V-Mail ($3-5)

Postcards

POSTCARDS-served as another important reminder to Americans of the reasons their country was now fighting. Their purpose was quite simple- to demonize or poke fun at the Axis powers while simultaneously glorifying the "V for Victory" symbol. Despite America's late entry into a war that had already been raging for over two full years, the attack on Pearl Harbor triggered an almost immediate production of these patriotic, humorous and often outlandish postcards. Standard size is 3 1/2" x 5 1/2." Major suppliers of "V" cards were E.C. Kropp Co. and Tichnor Bros. *Assorted Postcards ($10-15)*

"V for Victory" Collectibles

Assorted Postcards ($10-15)

Assorted Postcards ($10-15)

Postal Covers

11

POSTAL COVERS- Spanning from 1941 to the war's end, over 1,000 different cover styles with the "V" or "Victory" were produced. They sported wartime illustrations and captions with "V for Victory." These ever-popular covers proclaimed America's resolve to the soldiers abroad, war workers in the factories and families on the homefront, that Americans backed the war effort. 3 1/2" x 6 3/8" and up to 3 1/2" x 9" in size, among their designers were prominent illustrators such as Crosby, Staehle, Knapp, Fluegal, Minkus and others. *Assorted Postal Covers ($15-20)*

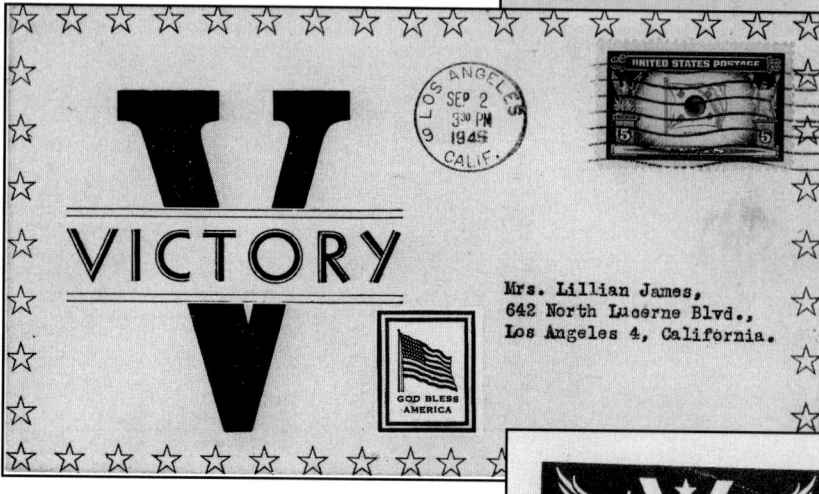

Assorted Postal Covers ($15-20)

Assorted Postal Covers ($15-20)

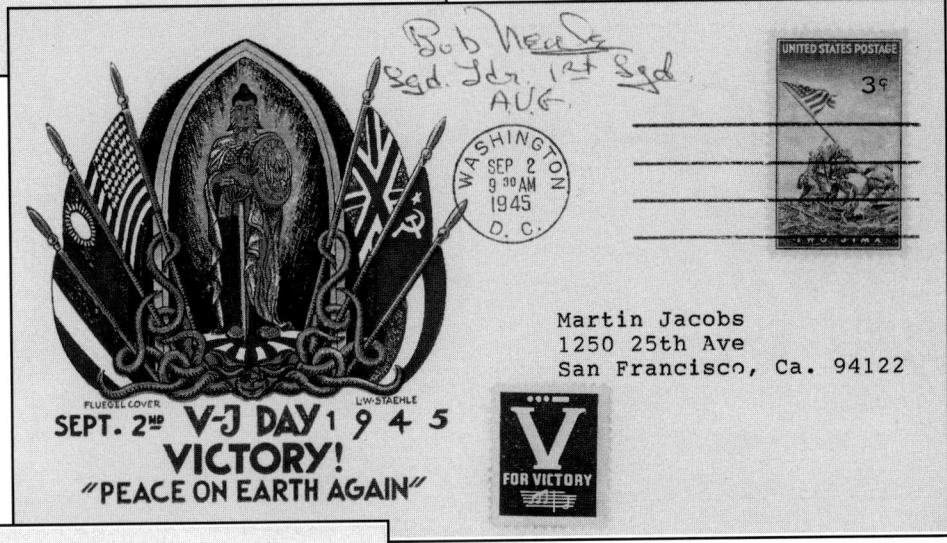

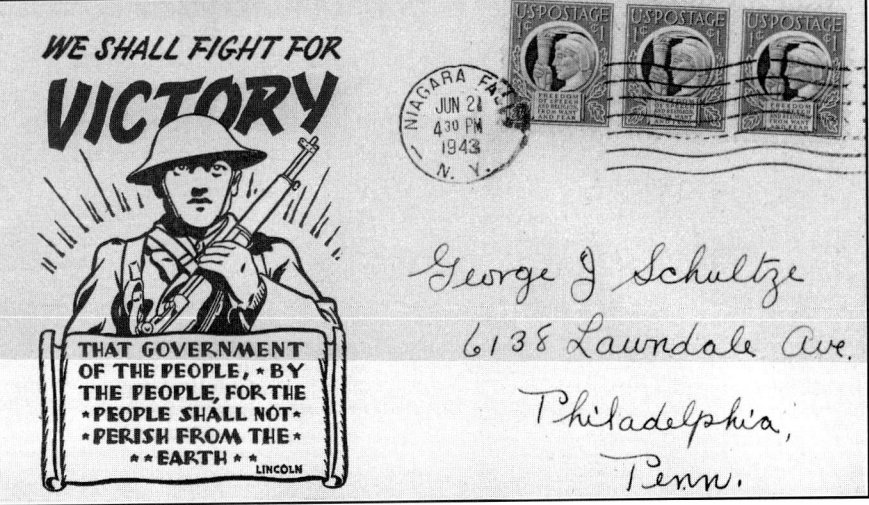

14   "V for Victory" Collectibles

Assorted Postal Covers ($15-20)

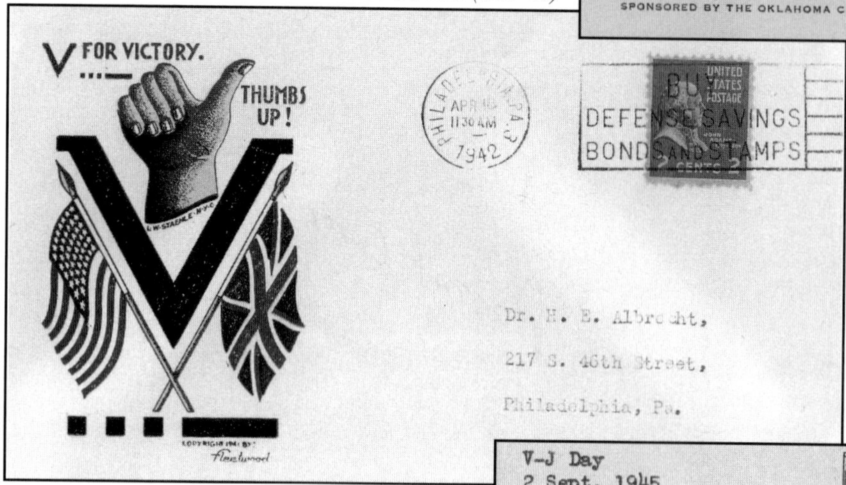

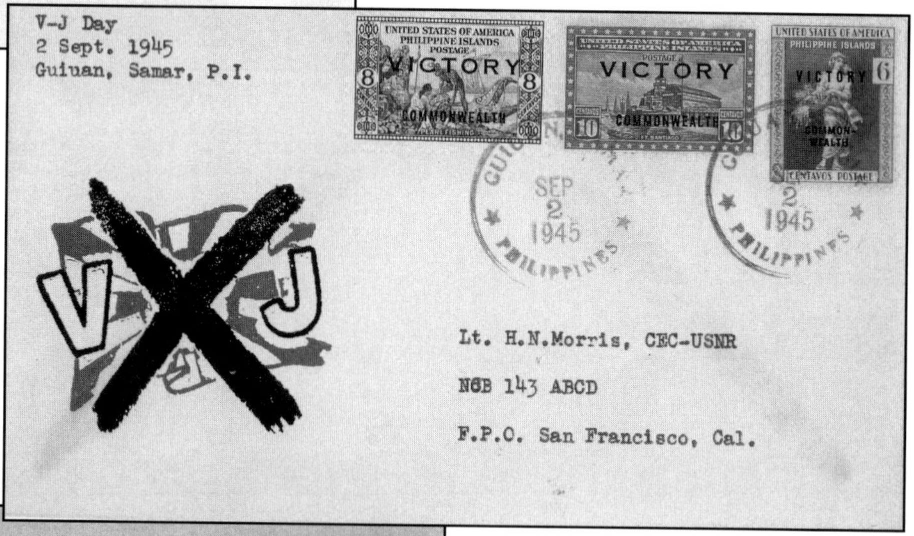

Stamps and Bonds

Poster Stamps ($5-10)

Back of truck trailer, Charlotte, North Carolina, March 1943.

"V for Victory" Collectibles

Block of Stamps ($20-25)

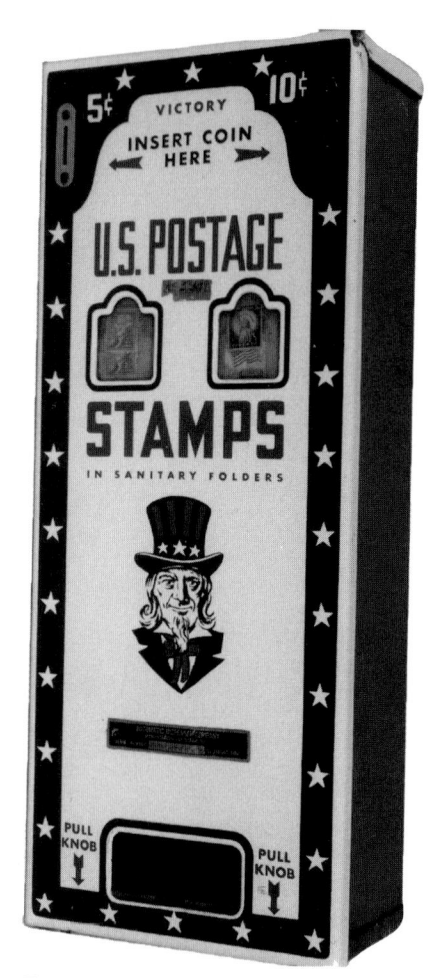

Postage Machine ($400-450)

Stamp ($2-3)

Stamp ($2-3)

Stamp ($2-3)

Stamp ($2-3)

Savings Bond Holders ($15-20)

18

Linens

Silk Handkerchief ($25-35)

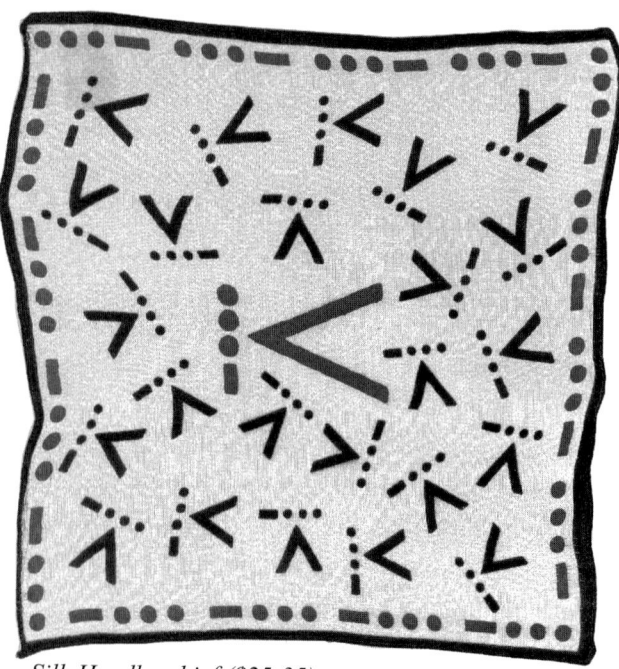

Silk Handkerchief ($25-35)

Silk Handkerchief ($25-35)

"V for Victory" Collectibles

19

Cloth Napkin Set ($45-55)

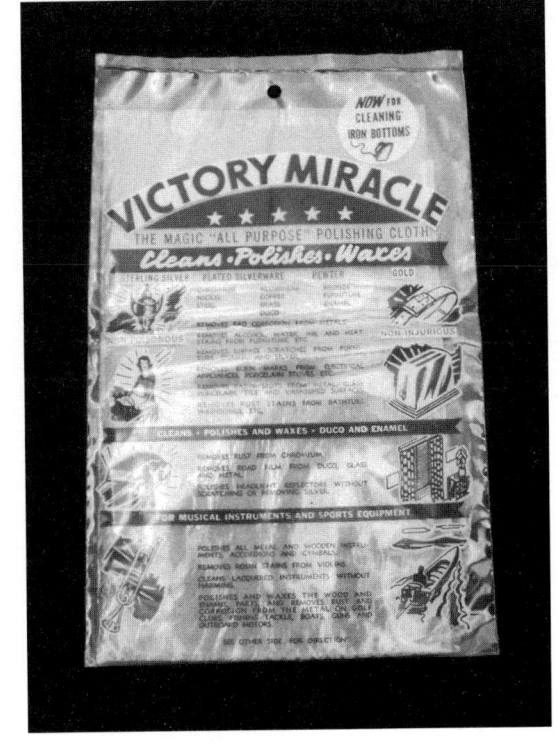

Polish Cloth ($20-25)

Silk Handkerchief ($25-35)

Cloth Coasters ($15-20)

Silk Handkerchief ($25-35)

Banners

($45-55)

($65-75)

($55-65)

Millions of men were shipped overseas to fight in the war and families left stateside proclaimed their participation in the war by displaying the "family member in-the-service" banner. The red, white and blue silk banners usually were hung in the front window of a family's home. The banners had a blue star for each family member in the service.

($55-65)

($45-55)

($45-55)

"V for Victory" Collectibles 21

Assorted Banners ($35-45)

Greeting Cards

No occasion went unnoticed without sending a "V" greeting card to a sweetheart in the service. Shown are examples of birthday, Christmas, Valentine's Day and others. Sizes vary from 4 1/2" to 6 1/2." *Assorted Greeting Cards ($15-20)*

"V for Victory" Collectibles

Assorted Greeting Cards ($15-20)

"V for Victory" Collectibles

Assorted Greeting Cards ($15-20)

Victory Gardens

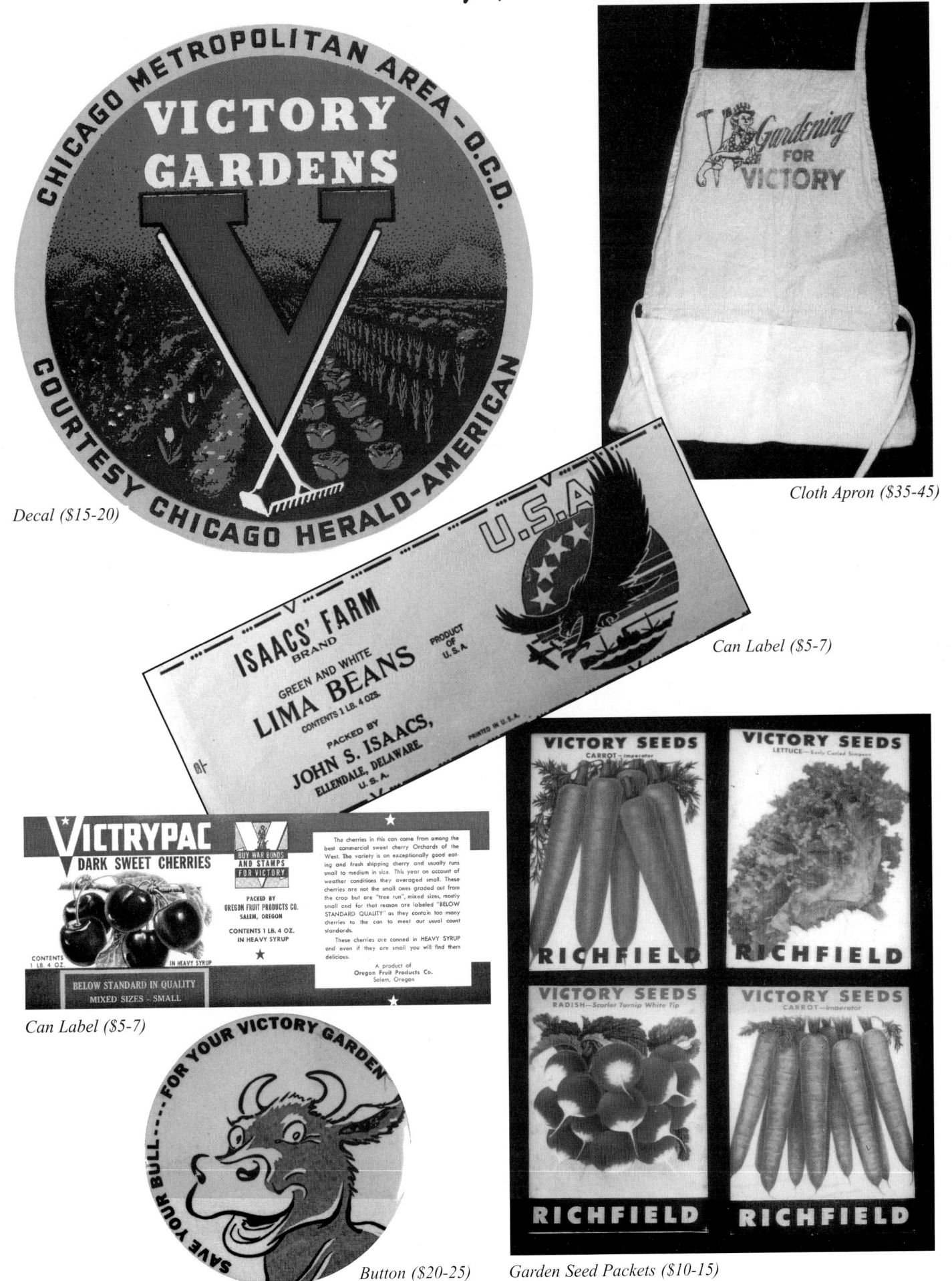

Decal ($15-20)

Cloth Apron ($35-45)

Can Label ($5-7)

Can Label ($5-7)

Button ($20-25)

Garden Seed Packets ($10-15)

26   *"V for Victory" Collectibles*

Sticker ($10-15)

Circular ($5-7)

Booklet ($15-20)

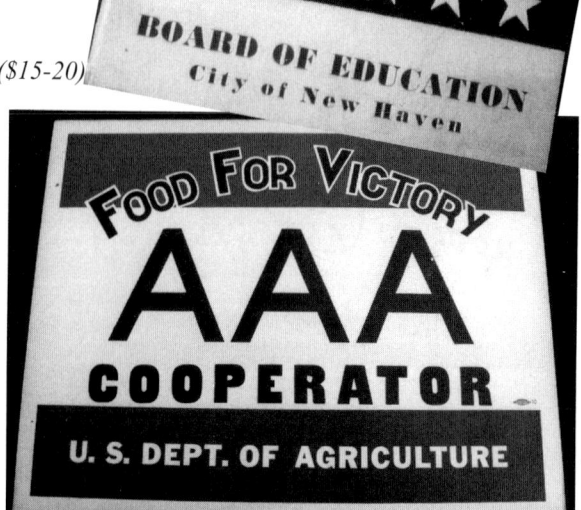

Poster ($65-75)

Sticker ($7-10)

Victory Gardens

Assorted Booklets ($20-25)

Garden Nozzle ($20-25)

Sign on Wilshire Boulevard, Los Angles, California, February 1943

28

Ticket ($55-65)

Ticket ($20-25)

Ticket ($150-175)

Flannel Jersey ($1,000-1,500)

Scorecard ($75-100)

Scorecard ($75-100)

"V for Victory" Collectibles

Scorecard ($75-100)

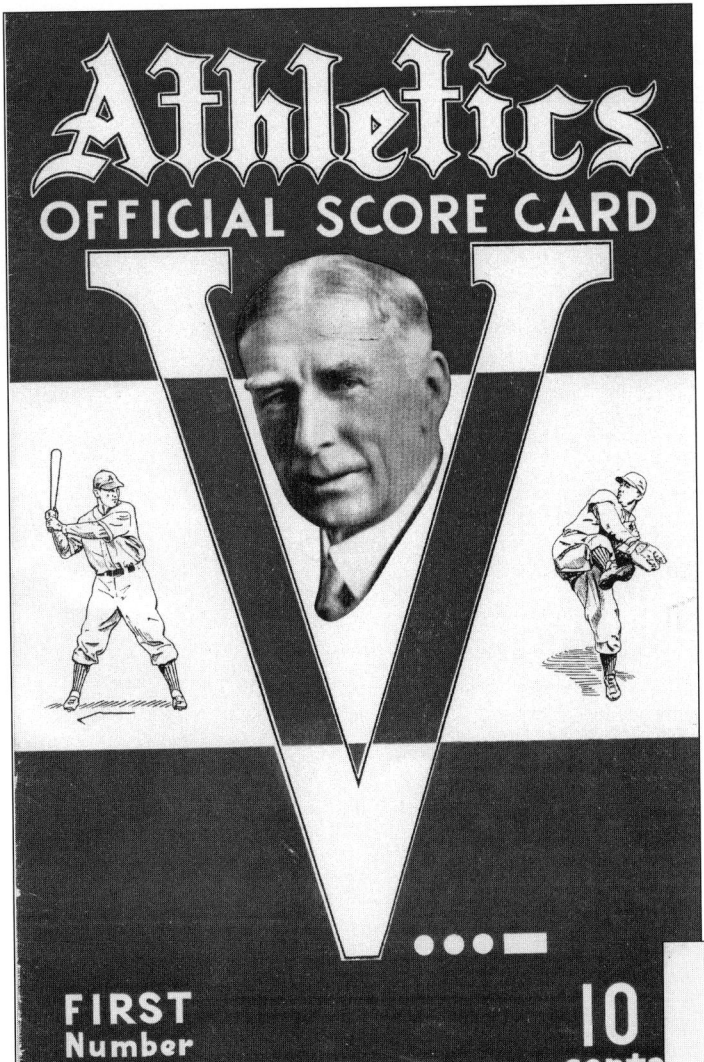

Scorecard ($75-100)

Scorecard ($75-100)

Program ($50-75)

Movies

War movie posters incorporated the "V" and word "Victory" with the morse code and were highly visible. They touted themes of the lurking danger of espionage and reminded Americans not to forget our "Victories." Standard poster sizes were 20" x 30" and 30" x 40."
Assorted Movie Posters ($175-225)

Sailors listening to the end of the war declaration.

Assorted Movie Posters ($175-225)

32

Books, Booklets, Magazines and Comics

Assorted Booklets ($20-25)

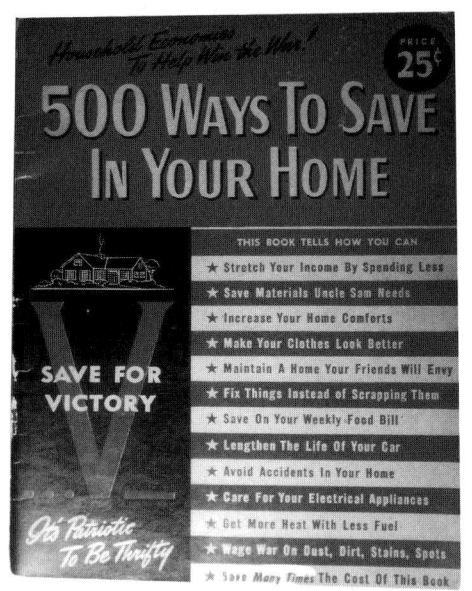

"V for Victory" Collectibles   33

Assorted Booklets ($20-25)

"V for Victory" Collectibles

Bookmark ($5-7)

Assorted Booklets ($20-25)

Books, Booklets, Magazines and Comics

35

Assorted Magazines ($15-20)

"V for Victory" Collectibles

Hardcover Book ($25-35)

Magazine ($15-20)

Hardcover Book ($25-35)

Magazine ($15-20)

Books, Booklets, Magazines and Comics 37

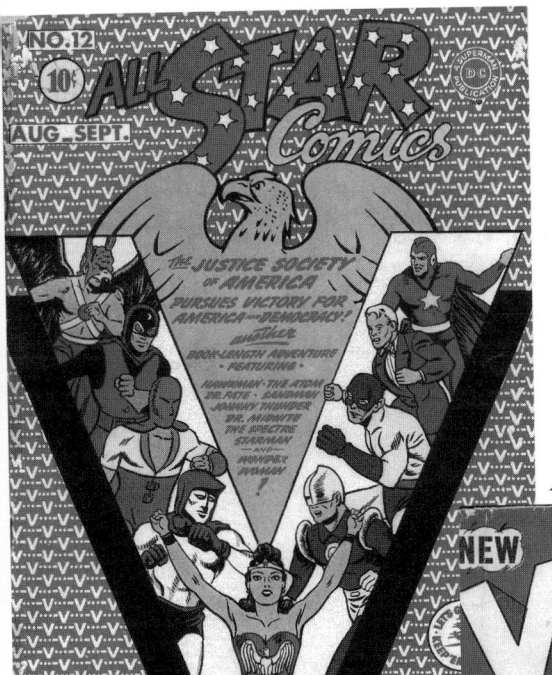

Assorted Comics ($175-225)

Products

Drinking-Straw/Wrapper ($5-7)

Leather Gloves ($55-65)

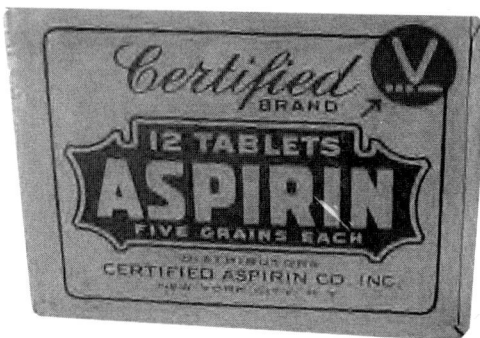

Aspirin Box ($15-20)

Paper Napkin ($5-7)

Beer Bottle ($35-45)

Glass Jar ($25-35)

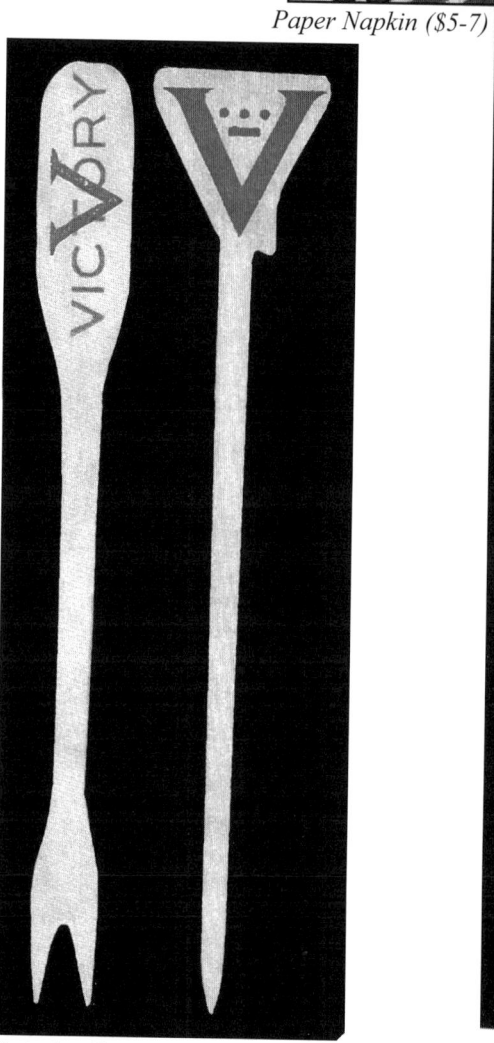

Swizzles ($10-15)

Milk Bottle ($100-125)

"V" for Victory Collectibles 39

Beverage Bottle ($10-15)

Hair Pin Box ($15-20)

Heel Plates ($25-35)

Light Bulb Fixture ($10-15)

Comb Display ($65-75)

Dolly Pins ($35-45)

Billfold Display ($75-85)

40　　　　　　　　　　　　　　　　　　　　　　"V" for Victory Collectibles

Children's Overalls ($75-85)

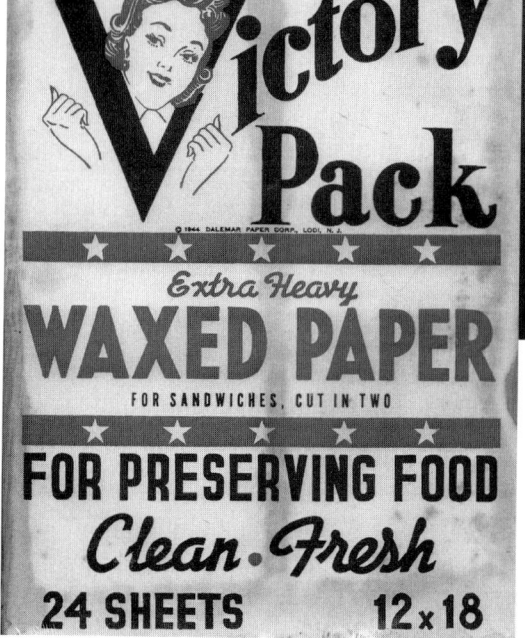

Cardboard Box ($35-45)

Garden Spray ($35-45)

Wax Paper ($35-45)

Candy ($45-55)

Child's Neck Tie ($45-55)

Jewelry, Buttons, Patches and Ribbons

Sterling Bracelet ($50-75)

Collecting jewelry is a fascinating way to preserve a unique piece of history from WWII, and the items are highly prized today. In the short span of ten years, since the 50th anniversary of WWII, I've amassed some 500 "V" pins denoting the famous "V for Victory" symbol.

My first "V" collectible pin was a Lone Ranger Victory Club tin fold-back I wore on my Navy jumper at the ripe age of 2. However, it was the women that were left behind when their men went to war who showed their patriotism in a variety of ways--among them the accessories they wore with their clothing. It was quite fashionable to wear a "V" or "Victory" pin--whether you worked in a factory, department store, in a school or within the home. Many pins were mass produced by US manufacturers and government agencies. Yet, there were also those specially hand-crafted "V" pins produced in small towns across the country. They are one-of-a-kind pieces and are highly sought after by collectors.

Today, finding a "V" or "Victory" sweetheart pin is a valued treasure. Not because of its intrinsic value, but rather due to the historical significance it bears to our last great patriotic war. Another reason is the beauty of the "V" pins--in service pins, wings of love, pendants, necklaces, bracelets and broaches. There are over 300 known variations and materials used to fashion these "V" pins, and many of these pieces are incorporated with the morse code (dot-dot-dot-dash) symbol for "Victory." They also range in size, quality, design and accouterments from a single brass pin to bakelite, sterling, pot metal, marquisate, pewter, celluloid, copper, leather, wood, shell, plastic, gold-filled, gold-plated or gold-washed. Generally, they are adorned with the symbolic USA or British flags, eagles, rhinestones, amethysts, pearls or even diamonds. Company names- Trifari, Coro, "LN" Co. and Accessocraft were known to stamp their logo on the back on the pins.

The small celluloid pin-back button also made a bold statement! They proliferated the war effort with catchy phrases like: "If it's V, it's for Me!" "V for Volunteers," "Jr. Victory Corps," "Plant a Victory Garden," "Ships for Victory," "Remember Pearl Harbor-On to Victory," "V for Allied Victory," "V-E Day" and "V-J Day."

There have been millions of words written about WWII, but for me, there will be only one indelible shining symbol- an icon that will always remind me of the war effort: The prolific "V" pin!

Sterling Bracelet ($125-150)

Sterling Bracelet ($125-150)

Sonja Henie "V" Pin

One of the most greatly coveted "V" pins is a 2" copper pin--a silhouette of Sonja Henie, the popular Olympic ice-skater who charmed Hitler at the 1936 Olympics and went on the be a successful Hollywood movie star. This particular souvenir pin was sold throughout the war at her touring ice skating shows around the country. Once you take a closer look at this pin, with a little imagination, one may see some resemblance to Henie's face, hair-style and Olympic-style costume. *($125-150)*

42   "V" for Victory Collectibles

Plastic ($35-45)

Sterling/ Rhinestones ($150-175)

Beaded ($35-45)

Plastic ($35-45)

Sterling/ Rhinestones ($150-175)

Plastic ($25-35)

Sterling ($150-175)

Pot Metal ($25-35)

Wood ($35-45)

Plastic ($35-45)

Jewelry, Buttons, Patches and Ribbons

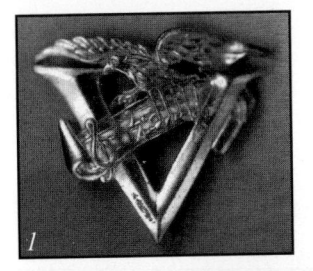

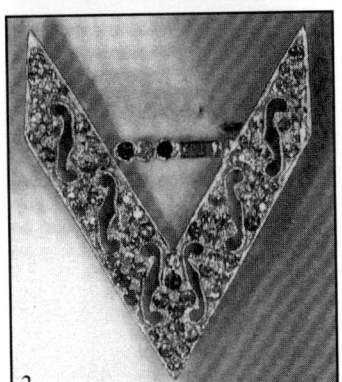

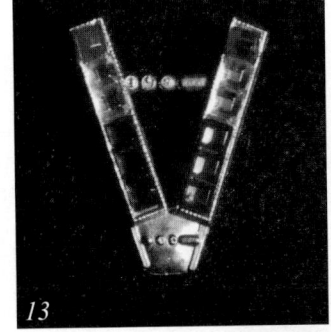

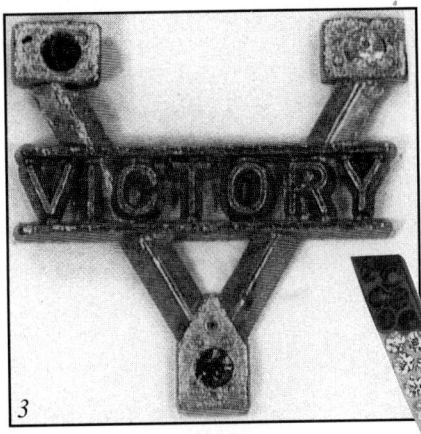

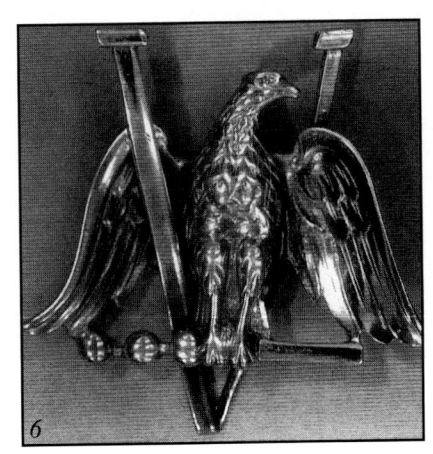

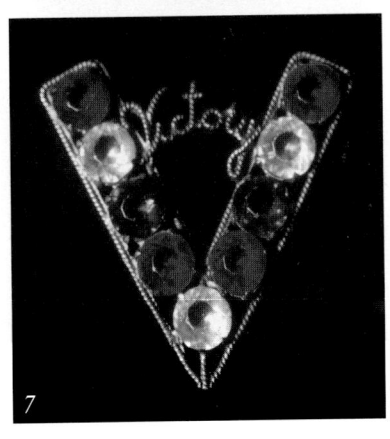

1-Gold Plated ($75-100), 2-Sterling/ Jeweled ($45-65), 3-Plastic ($55-65), 4-Sterling/ Jeweled ($55-65), 5-Pot Metal ($45-55), 6-Sterling ($75-85), 7-Sterling/ Jeweled ($200-225), 8-Sterling ($75-85), 9-Sterling ($100-125), 10-Sterling ($55-65), 11-Pot Metal ($55-65), 12-Nickel ($25-35), 13-Sterling Jeweled ($45-55), 14-Broach/ Jeweled ($250-300), 15-Plastic ($35-45).

Bakelite ($400-450)

Hollywood celebrates the end of World War II.

Bakelite ($150-175)

Lucite ($35-45)

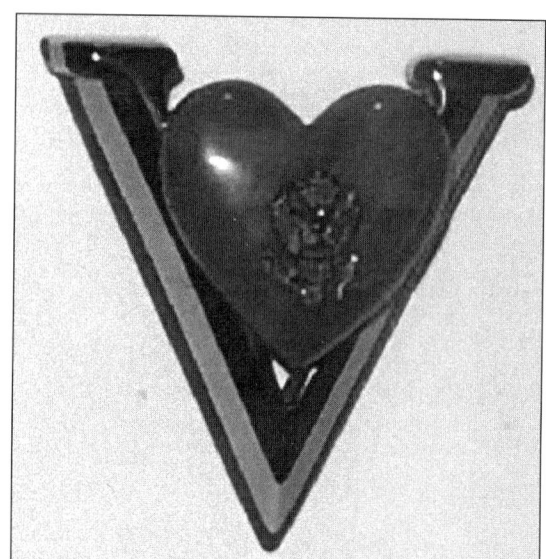

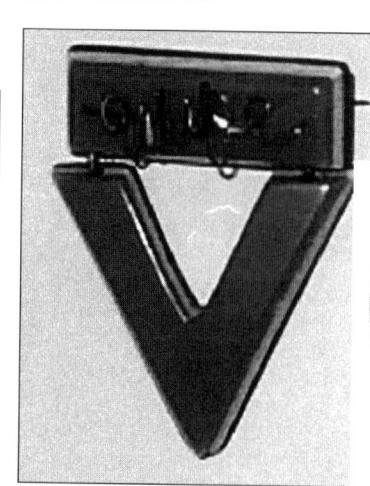

Bakelite ($150-175)

Bakelite ($400-450)

Bakelite ($400-450)

Jewelry, Buttons, Patches and Ribbons

Assorted Celluloid Buttons ($10-35)

46   *"V" for Victory Collectibles*

Key Tag ($15-20)

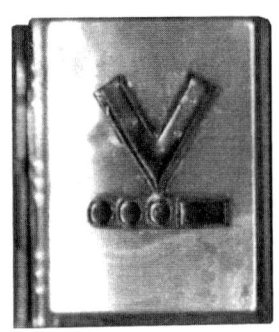

Locket ($75-100)

Felt Patch ($25-35)

Bobbie Pins ($20-25)

Cloth Patch ($25-35)

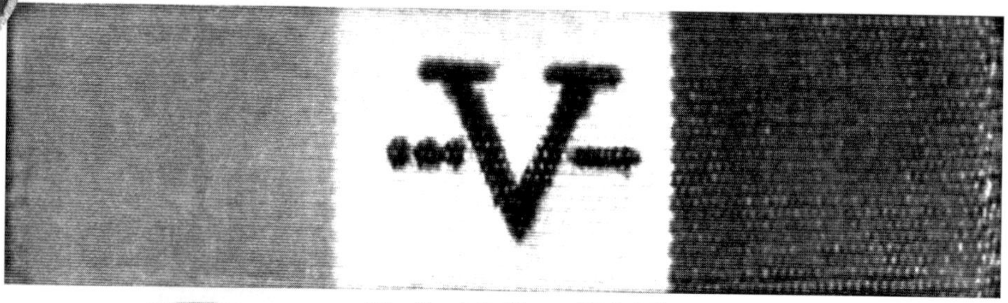

Pin-Back Ribbon ($25-35)

Embroidered Patch ($35-45)

Embroidered Patch ($35-45)

Cloth Ribbon ($15-20)

Cinderellas, Stickers and Decals

Cinderellas were styled after postage stamps and came in a multitude of sizes and shapes. Windows all over America were plastered with them reminding our nation not to forget Pearl Harbor and to accept nothing less than Victory. They were typically lithographed on adhesive paper or made into decals, stickers, stamps and labels and then affixed to envelopes, stationary, bookcovers, postcards or any smooth surface to show support for the war effort. *Assorted Stickers ($3-7)*

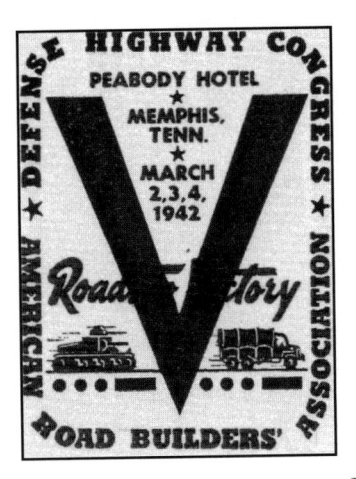

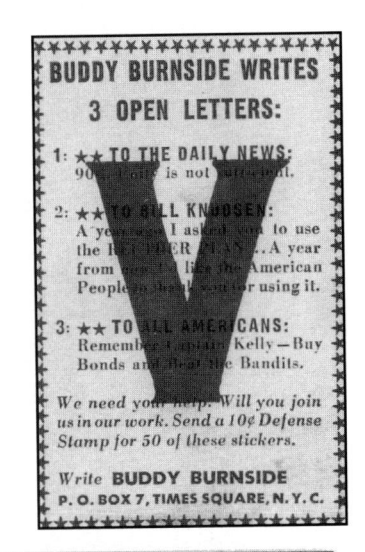

48 "V" for Victory Collectibles

Decal ($7-10)

Sticker ($20-25)

Label ($7-10)

Labels ($1-2 each)

Decal ($15-20)

Decal ($7-10)

Sticker Box ($7-10)

Sticker ($2-3)

Cinderellas, Stickers and Decals 49

Sticker ($5-7)

Decal ($5-7)

Sticker ($10-15)

Decal ($10-15)

Sticker ($10-15)

Decal ($7-10)

Decal ($20-25)

Sticker ($5-7)

Decal ($10-15)

Decal ($15-20)

Label ($2-3)

Stamp ($2-3)

Sticker ($5-7)

Cinderellas, Stickers and Decals

51

Decal ($20-25)

Decal ($15-20)

Decal ($20-25)

Decal ($15-20)

Decal ($20-25)

Assorted Posters ($75-225)

Posters

53

Assorted Posters ($75-225)

54   *"V" for Victory Collectibles*

Assorted Posters ($75-225)

Posters

Assorted Posters ($75-225)

"V" for Victory Collectibles

Assorted Posters ($75-225)

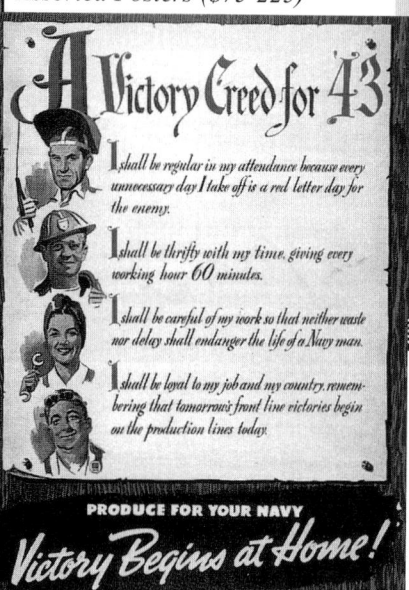

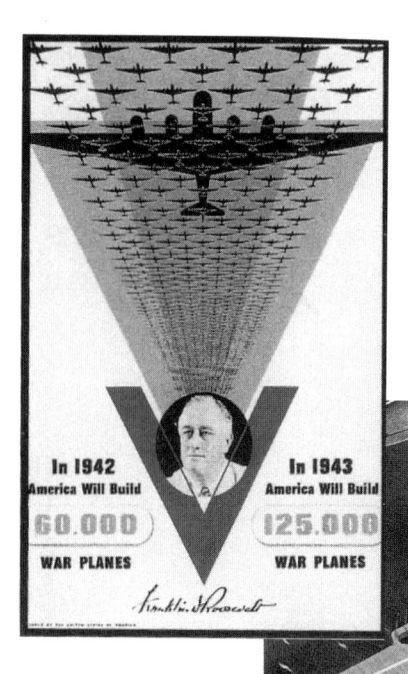

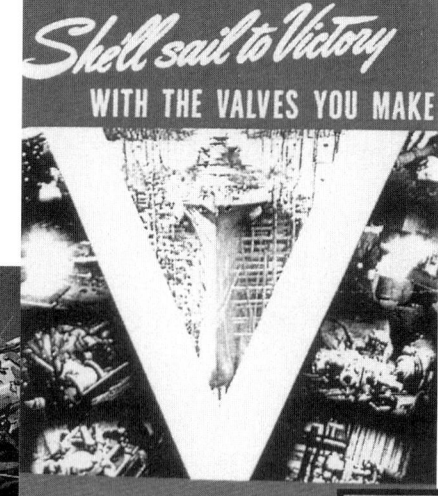

Toys and Playthings

Puzzles ($50-75)

World War II inspired widespread patriotism that resulted in the mass production of wonderful toys and games. The "V for Victory" slogan was immortalized on every item imaginable.

Major suppliers including F.A.O. Swartz Co., Louis Marx and Co., Wyandotte, Wolverine, American Toy Works, Reed Co., Whitman Publishing, Lido Toys, Milton Bradley Co. and Parker Bros., produced puzzles, coloring books, painting sets, pistols, rifles, model airplanes and ships, board games, card games, punch boards, banks and paper dolls for children. Soon after the outbreak of war, many toys and games were constructed of "nonessential materials" such as wood, plastic and leather instead of steel, aluminum, rubber and other critical materials that were required for life rafts, bomb parts, radios and metal shells for the war effort.

Plywood Puzzle ($50-75)

58   "V" for Victory Collectibles

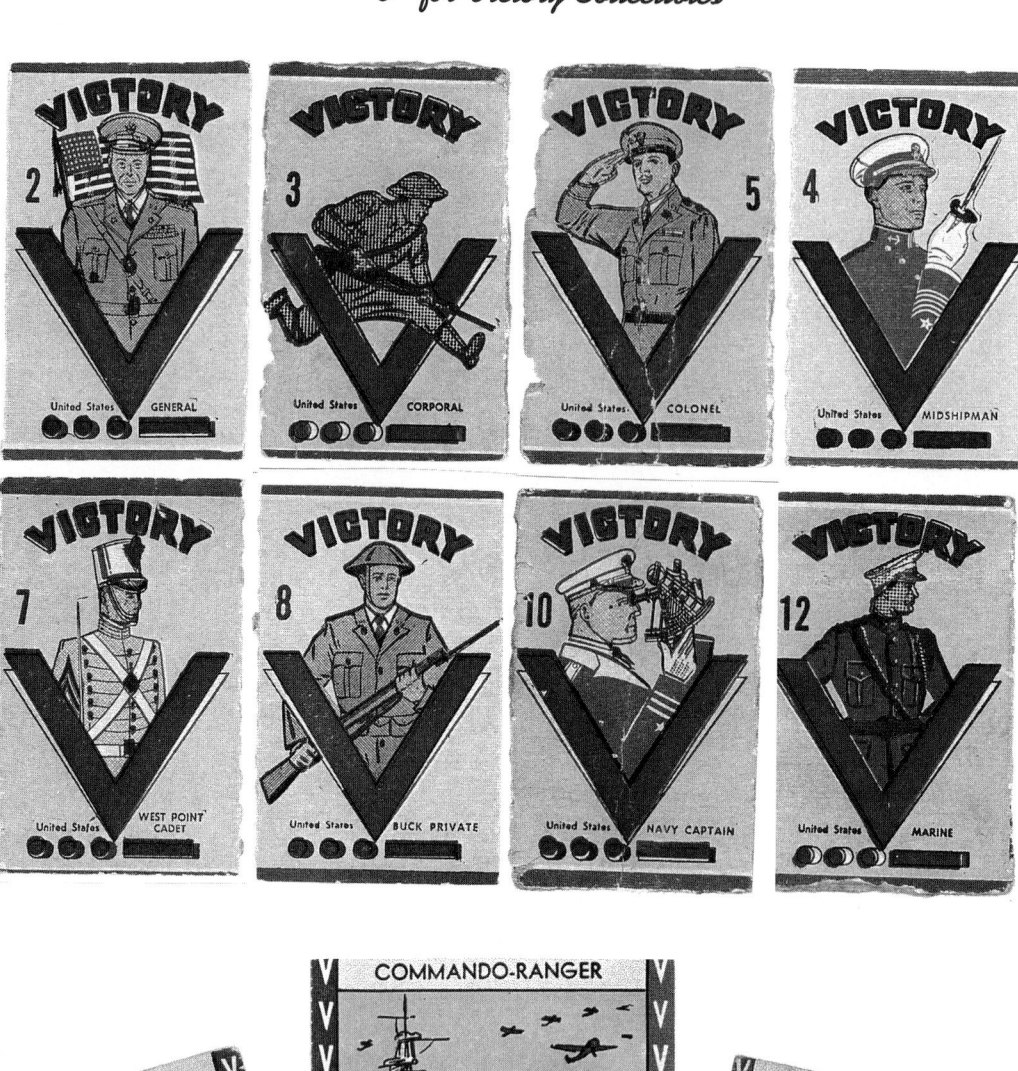

Assorted Gum Cards ($50-75)

Board Game ($75-85)

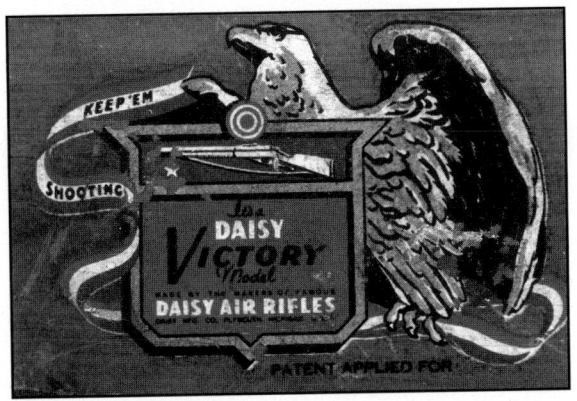

Toy Rifle ($200-225)

Toy Soldiers ($100-125)

Playthings ($100-125)

Playthings ($125-150)

Toy ($75-85)

Toy ($55-65)

Toy ($65-75)

Toy ($45-55)

Toy ($45-55)

Toy ($100-125)

Toys and Playthings

Assorted Card Decks ($75-125)

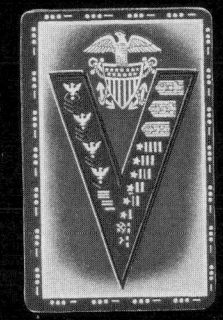

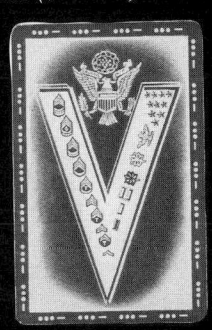

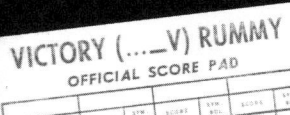

Dart Board ($50-75)

THE LONE RANGER VICTORY CORPS

Put 'er there, Pardner!

You are now a full-fledged member of THE LONE RANGER VICTORY CORPS. Let me congratulate you on your willingness to do your share for our great country!

Enclosed is your official "Victory Corps" material, including the Membership-Identification card, your Instructions and the official Insignia which will identify you as a full-fledged member of the "Victory Corps".

Ours is a serious responsibility that can and will make a real contribution to our country's all-out Victory effort. There are many jobs that the Lone Ranger Victory Corps can and will do to help, such as:

SALVAGE OF WASTEPAPER, SALVAGE OF RUBBER, SALVAGE OF METALS, DISTRIBUTION OF GOVERNMENT LITERATURE, GARDENING, CONSERVATION OF FOOD AND POWER, AIR RAID PRECAUTIONS IN YOUR OWN HOME, ETC., ETC.

Special messages will be given on these and other jobs. So be sure to keep tuned to the Lone Ranger for your official instructions.

The Lone Ranger

A 2186

Lone Ranger Victory Corps Kit ($1,000-1,500)

No. 275708

This is to Certify that the Bearer

(Member must sign here)

is a duly authorized member of the
LONE RANGER VICTORY CORPS
and solemnly pledges to observe all duties thereof

The Lone Ranger

COPYRIGHT 1942, THE LONE RANGER, INC.

★ PLEDGE TO THE FLAG ★

"I pledge allegiance to the Flag of the United States of America, and to the Republic for which it stands, One Nation indivisible, with liberty and justice for all."

Toys and Playthings 63

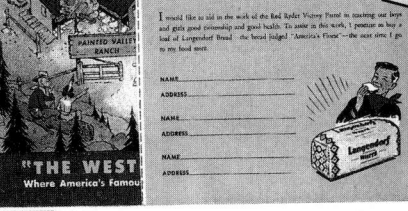

Red Ryder Victory Kit ($1,000-1,500)

Tattoos ($45-55)

Dexterity Game ($50-75)

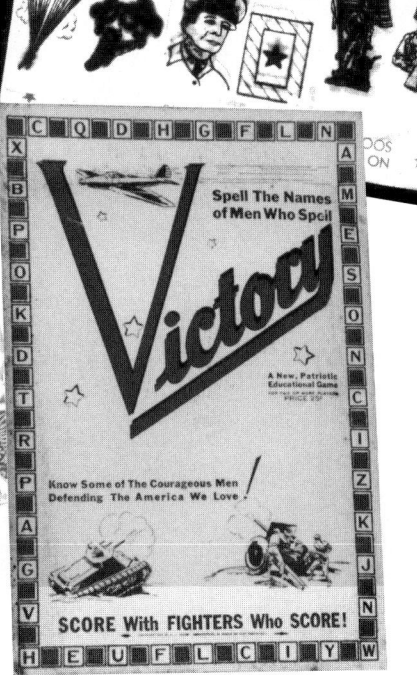

Board Game ($55-65)

Board Game ($65-75)

64   *"V" for Victory Collectibles*

Board Game ($75-100)

Puzzle ($50-75)

Puzzle ($50-75)

Dexterity Game ($50-75)

Toys and Playthings

Paper Dolls ($125-150)

Coloring Book ($55-65)

Coloring Book ($55-65)

Advertisements

Assorted Magazine Advertisements ($10-15)

Bridgeport, Connecticut, January 30, 1944.

"V" for Victory Collectibles

Assorted Magazine Advertisements ($10-15)

"V" for Victory Collectibles

Assorted Magazine Advertisements ($10-15)

Wings to Victory

Our widespread military and naval bases... our growing number of war-material factories... all are joined in one determination... VICTORY! All, too, are joined in an indispensable way by the nation's airlines... closely linking manufacturing and military efforts into one determined, impregnable front... a front where every minute gained is a victory won.

Add wings to your efforts in doing your part. As an example of the days and hours you can save, TWA can take you from Los Angeles to New York in less than 14 hours—from Chicago to New York in 3 hours and 33 minutes. And there are equally fast schedules between other important points. Save Time by Air!

TRANSCONTINENTAL & WESTERN AIR, INC.

TWA The Transcontinental Airline

V STANDS FOR VOLUME TOO!

Chevrolet, America's Foremost Volume Producer of Cars and Trucks, Has Devoted Its Skills and Resources to Victory!

America's armed might is making its inspiring strength felt round the globe. Wherever our soldiers take the field, Chevrolet-built equipment serves them well—for Chevrolet-built is quality-built.

And quantity-built as well, to supply constantly-expanding needs. In huge plants the nation over—now expanded even beyond their peacetime proportions—skilled Chevrolet craftsmen work diligently for our country.

Their output can be measured only in multi-millions of dollars—for censorship prohibits revelation of production figures.

Sleek-winged bombers now are powered by Chevrolet-built Pratt & Whitney airplane engines.

Rugged, durable Army trucks which Chevrolet has engineered and built in multiple thousands for the past many months are aiding America's fighting men in every branch of the Service, everywhere in the world.

Armor-piercing shells, produced in vast quantities by Chevrolet, scream defiance wherever man challenges freedom. An ever-increasing number of aluminum forgings for airplanes... together with many other different kinds of parts for other war producers, both within and without General Motors... are flowing from the great Chevrolet factories.

As our armed forces increase, so is Chevrolet bolstering its gigantic production army. Employment is increasing with each passing week. The contribution of these craftsmen to the national war program is tremendous now and will continue to grow day after day.

Accustomed to thinking and operating on a volume basis, Chevrolet proudly presents this report to America.

CHEVROLET DIVISION OF **GENERAL MOTORS** — AMERICA'S FOREMOST VOLUME PRODUCER OF CARS AND TRUCKS

How War Bonds Buy Victory

- Every time you buy a War Bond, you are bringing Victory just a little closer.
- War Bond holders own a share in the greatest warplanes the world has seen.
- War Bonds mean "Fire-Power"—such as the aircraft cannon Oldsmobile builds.
- More "Fire-Power!" These are hard-hitting, Oldsmobile-built cannon for tanks.
- And shell by the million! Oldsmobile has been turning 'em out for two years.
- War Bond dollars back up our fighters—training, equipping, supplying them.
- They fight with your dollars, with guns and ships your Bonds help to buy.
- Even if you don't work on war production, let your War Bond dollars work for you.
- Some day... VICTORY! And you'll get back every War Bond dollar, plus interest.

HOW OLDSMOBILE BUILDS FOR VICTORY!

KEEP 'EM FIRING!

THE FACTS AND FIGURES, such as can be revealed, tell an impressive story. Oldsmobile swung into volume production of war equipment as early as April, 1941, nearly two years ago. Since then *millions* of high-explosive shell and armor-piercing shot... *thousands* of fast-firing automatic cannon for fighter planes... *thousands* of long-range, high-velocity cannon for tanks, have flowed from the Oldsmobile production lines. Working in close co-operation with more than 130 sub-contractors, Oldsmobile today has reached a peak of war production volume that once would have seemed impossible.

But the facts don't tell all. Let's remember, it's the men who use the weapons we build and buy, who will bring us Victory. So, let's build an *extra* gun today... buy an *extra* Bond today... *for them!*

Oldsmobile was among the very first war producers to receive the Army-Navy "E" award for outstanding production. That is the greatest distinction we could ask today, because—Victory is our Business!

"You bet, War Bonds work for Victory"

THEY SUPPLY RADIO EQUIPMENT FOR INVASION

"Take it from me, the speed of the invasion of Europe and the Pacific islands would have been almost impossible without the split-second coordination of radio to back up the courage of our fighters. But your War Bonds are still needed—and urgently—to make this Victory final and complete."

RCA 1919–1944 25 YEARS OF PROGRESS RADIO AND ELECTRONICS

Victory will bring the Boys back home

RCA WILL MAKE GREAT RADIOS AND PHONOGRAPHS

Yes, it will be a great day when brand new 1940-X RCA radios and radio-phonographs are unpacked in American homes... bringing even finer tone and more beautiful cabinets than ever before. Watch for the RCA Super FM circuit... for the great RCA television sets that are in the offing.

While anticipating the great days of peace RCA will continue to produce radios, radar, submarine detectors and other electronic equipment for planes... tanks... ships... of the U.S. Armed Forces.

RADIO CORPORATION OF AMERICA
RCA VICTOR DIVISION, CAMDEN, N. J.
LEADS THE WAY... in Radio... Television... Tubes... Phonographs... Records... Electronics

TUNE IN RCA's radio program, "The Music America Loves Best"... every Sunday, 4:30 P.M., EWT, NBC network.

Advertisements

Boy Scouts in Albuquerque, New Mexico.

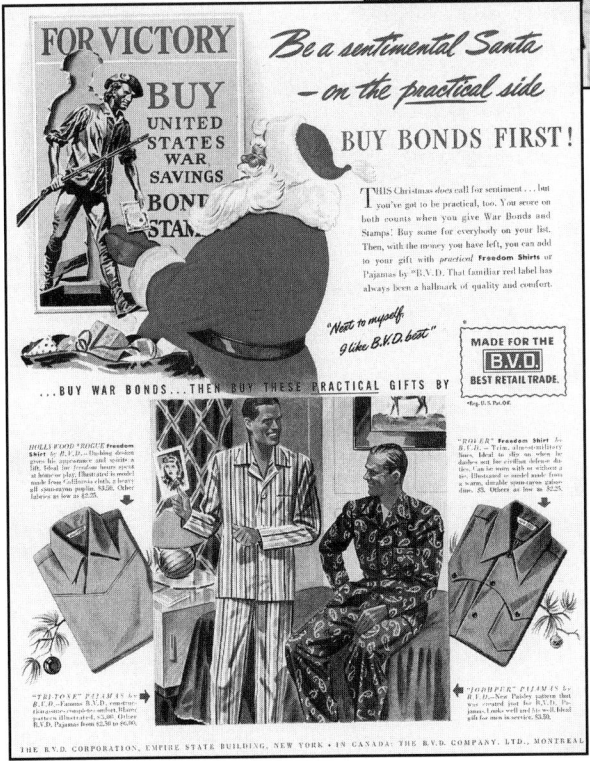

Assorted Magazine Advertisements ($10-15)

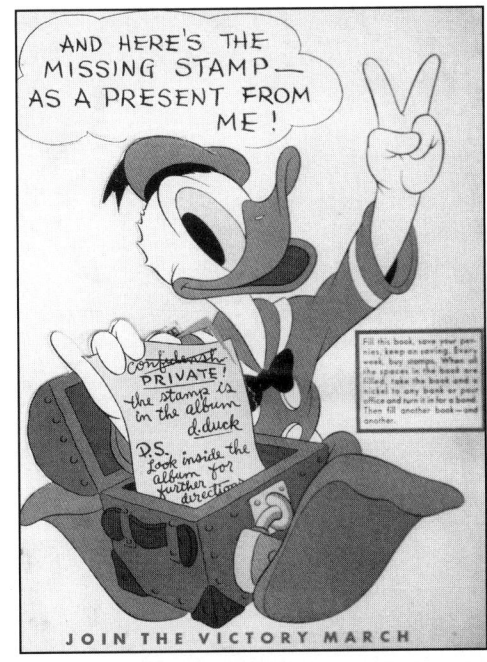

70   "V" for Victory Collectibles

Victory Vitamin "C"

During the war, Florida Grapefruit Juice sponsored the clever Victory Vitamin "C" advertising campaign for our troops and general public:

"Victory Vitamin 'C' helps keep those burly bodies in perfect fighting trim. And we're sparing no effort to give them all the Victory Vitamin 'C's' they need! Because everyday, Florida citrus fruits and countless cans of grapefruit juice are shipped to our fighting forces... At any rate you'll be glad to know it is reaching those guys who are teaching the Japs to 'Remember Pearl Harbor'...in a way they'll never forget!"

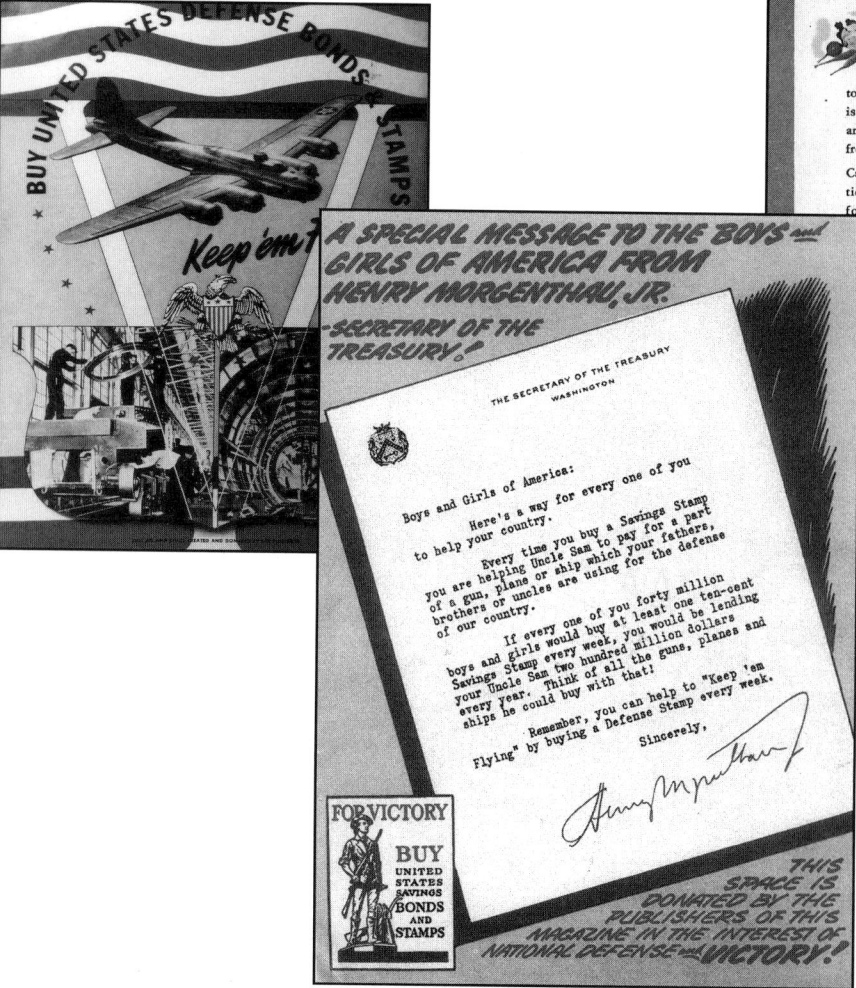

Assorted Magazine Advertisements ($10-15)

Miscellaneous

71

V-J Day, August 14, 1945.

Cloth Cap ($45-55)

Assorted Maps ($45-55)

Paper Hat ($35-45)

Ad Card ($10-15)

72   "V" for Victory Collectibles

Wooden License Plate ($35-45)

Metal License Plate Topper ($50-75)

Honolulu, Hawaii, V-J Day.

Metal License Plate ($75-100)

Metal License Plate Topper ($50-75)

Metal License Plate Topper ($175-225)

Metal License Plate Topper ($50-75)

Metal License Plate Topper ($50-75)

Metal License Plate Topper ($50-75)

Miscellaneous

Cardboard Box ($35-45)

Washboard ($65-75)

Cloth Armband ($45-55)

Statue ($65-75)

Ukulele ($1,000-1,500)

Times Square, New York City, August 14, 1945.

Victory Vanity ($50-75)

Milk Bottles ($125-150)

73

"V" for Victory Collectibles

Assorted Match Covers ($5-10)

Match Box ($15-20)

Matchbook Holder ($25-35)

Miscellaneous

Sugar Ration Spoon ($300-350)

Novelty Rings ($20-25)

Box of Sugar Cubes ($75-100)

Wood/ Cardboard ($125-150)

Ceramic Salt and Pepper Shakers ($50-75)

Wooden Serving Tray ($65-75)

Drinking Glasses ($50-75)

"V" for Victory Collectibles

Booklet ($20-25)

Metal Box ($50-75)

Board Game ($100-125)

Wooden Shelf ($55-25)

Cardboard Box ($35-45)

Miscellaneous

Leather Album ($20-25)

Cardboard Sign ($35-45)

Ceramic Lamp ($75-100)

Ration Book Holders ($5-20)

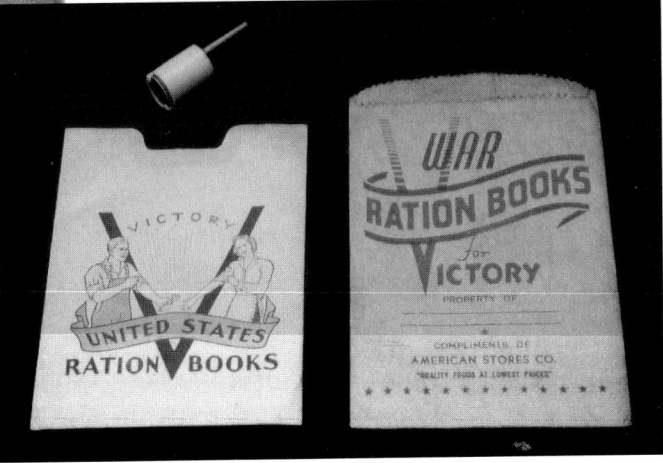

"V" for Victory Collectibles

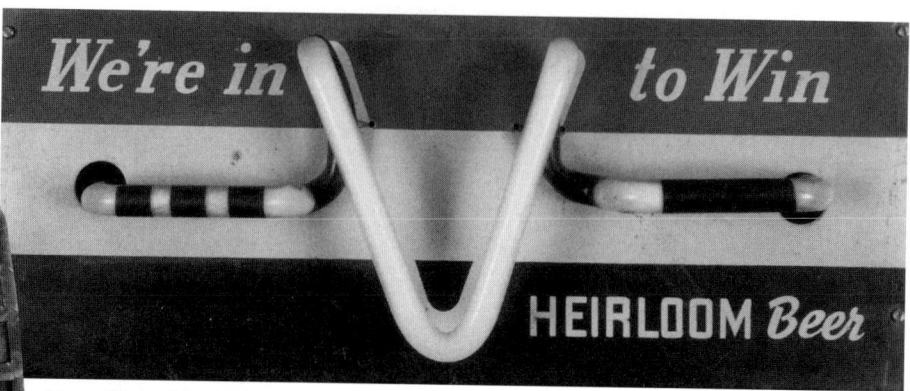

Neon Sign ($225-250)

Stained Glass ($55-65)

Porcelain Sign ($55-65)

Picture Frame Kit ($75-85)

Watch Display ($225-250)

Ceramic Bookends ($45-55)

Miscellaneous

79

Milk Bottle Caps ($5-10)

Ink Blotter ($25-35)

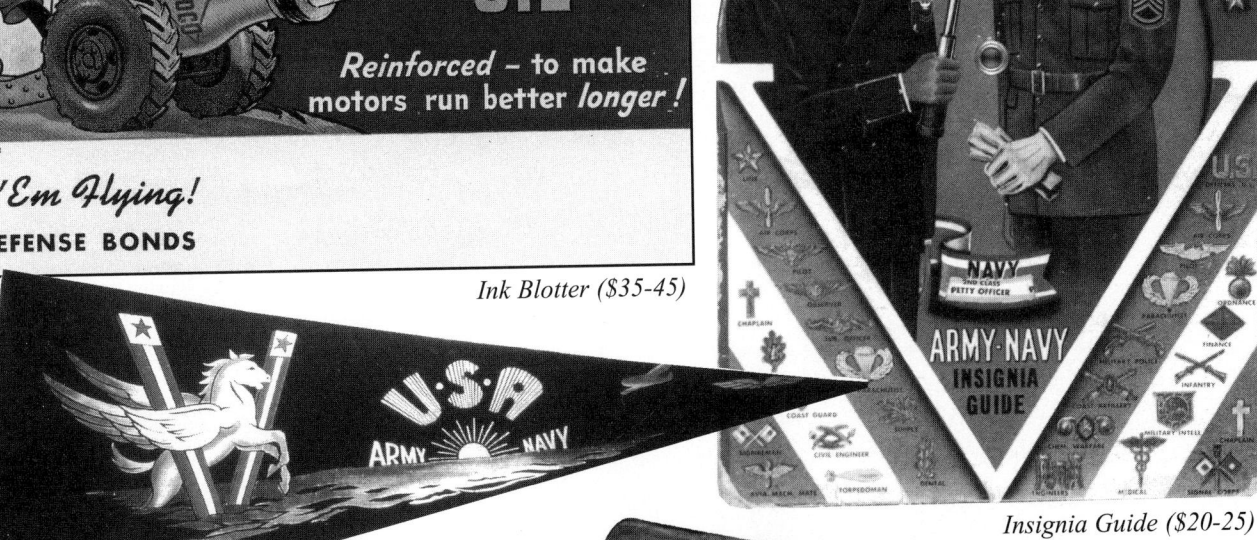

Ink Blotter ($35-45)

Insignia Guide ($20-25)

Belt Pennant ($50-75)

Cork Coaster ($7-10)

Wooden "Monkey" Box ($150-175)

"V" for Victory Collectibles

Drinking Glasses ($20-25)

Paper Cups ($10-15)

Drinking Glasses ($20-25)

Tin Can ($75-85)

Tin Can ($75-85)

Glass Pitcher and Glasses ($100-125)

Wooden Coasters ($35-45)

Miscellaneous

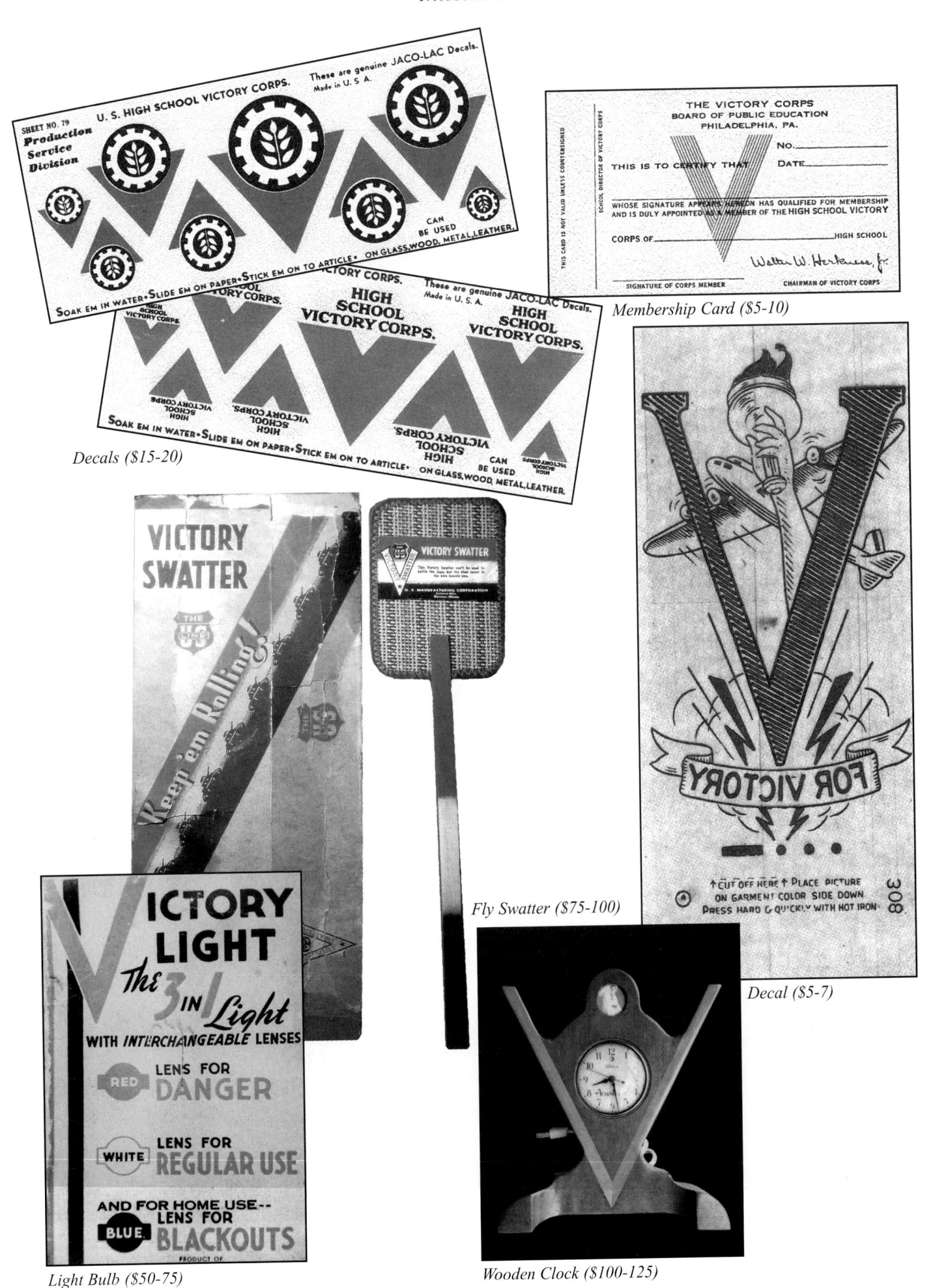

Decals ($15-20)

Membership Card ($5-10)

Fly Swatter ($75-100)

Decal ($5-7)

Light Bulb ($50-75)

Wooden Clock ($100-125)

81

Chalkware ($45-55)

Civilian Defense Helmet ($75-100)

Ink Blotter ($15-20)

Chalkware Statue ($55-65)

Spokane, Washington, V-J Day.

Miscellaneous

83

Paper Hat ($25-35)

Parade Float, Sacramento, California.

Child's Sweater ($35-45)

Cardboard Stand-up ($55-65)

Wooden Stamp ($35-45)

"V" for Victory Collectibles

Fluorescent Light ($150-175)

Woven Purse ($100-125)

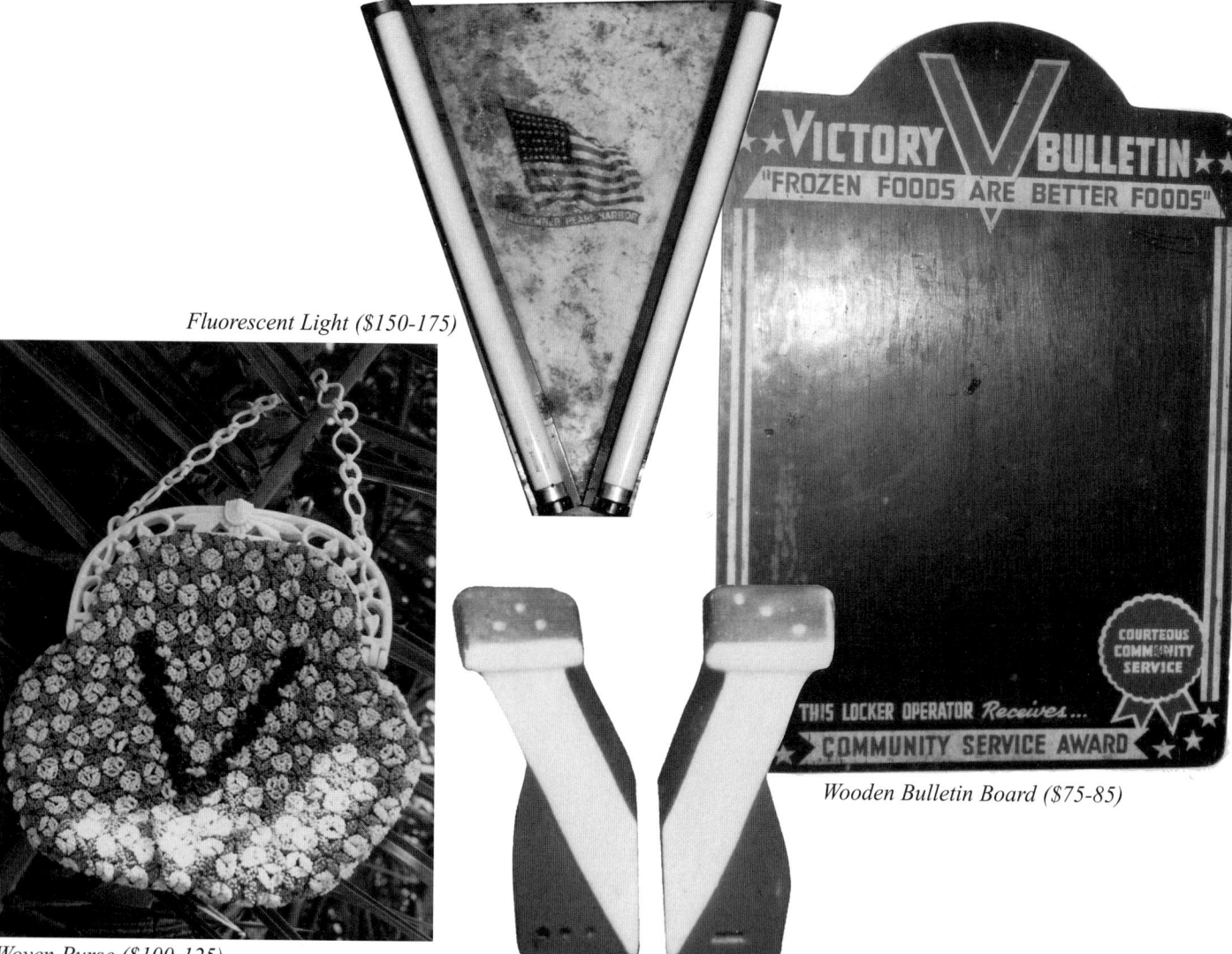

Salt and Pepper Shakers ($55-65)

Wooden Bulletin Board ($75-85)

Desk Clock ($75-85)

V-J Day on Market Street, San Francisco, California.

Chronology of Significant World War Two Victories

1942

April 18	U.S. (Doolittle) raid of B-25's bombers on Japan
May 4	Battle of Coral Sea (to May 8)
June 3	Battle of Midway (to June 6)
September 15	Battle of Papua, New Guinea (to January 22, 1943)
November 8	Allied forces invade North Africa (Operation Torch)
November 12	Battle of Guadalcanal (to November 15)

1943

May 7	Allied 18th Army group captures Tunis and Bizete
June 30	Operation Cartwheel (Rabaul) launched in Southwest Pacific
July 10	Allies invade Sicily (to August 17)
July 22	Palermo falls to U.S. Seventh Army
July 24	Allied bombers incinerate Hamburg (to August 3)
August 1	U.S. B-24's bomb Ploesti, Rumania (Operation Tidal Wave)
August 17	U.S. B-17's raid Schweinfurt and Regensburg
September 8	Eisenhower announces Italian surrender
September 9	Allies land at Salerno (to October 1)
November 1	U.S. Marines take Bouganville (Battle of Express Augusta Bay)
November 20	U.S. 2nd Marine Division lands on Tarawa (to November 23)

1944

January 20	Allied forces take Cassino (secured February 4)
January 31	U.S. Forces land o Kwajalein (to February 7)
February 29	U.S. Army forces take Admirality Islands
March 3	U.S. forces seize Manila from Japanese
March 11	U.S. Eighth Army units take Mindanao
June 6	Allies land at Normandy (Operation Overload)
June 15	U.S. Marines and Army invade Spain
June 19	Battle of Philippines Sea (Great Mariana's Turkey Shoot-to June 20)
June 22	U.S. forces take Cherbourg (secured July 13)
July 21	U.S. Marines and Army invade Guam (to August 13)
July 25	U.S. Third Army breaks out at Saint-Lo (Operation Cobra-to September 13)
August 15	Allies land in Southern France (Operation Anvil Dragon)
September 15	U.S. Marines land on Palau (to October 16)
October 23	Battle of Lyete Gulf (to October 26)
November 24	United States B-29's raid Japan
December 16	Battle of the Buldge and the Ardennes (to January 23, 1945)

1945

February 19	U.S. Marines land on Iwo Jima (to March 25)
April 1	U.S. Marines land on Okinawa (to May 21)
April 7	U.S. Navy planes sink the Japanese battleship Yamato in East China Sea
May 7	All German forces surrender unconditionally (2:41 a.m. at Rehims)
May 8	V-E Day (Unconditional surrender by the Germans)
August 14	Japan surrenders ending WWII
September 2	V-J Day (Japan signs instrument of surrender)

Victory Celebrations

Upon the ending of World War II in Europe in May 1945, the joyous victory celebrations that followed were tempered with the awareness that the war with Japan had yet to be won. On V-E Day, the bloody battle for Okinawa was raging. Burma and the Philippines were among the places where battles were still being fought. An invasion of Japan still loomed ominously on the horizon. Many of the troops who had survived the carnage of warfare against the Nazis were facing transfer to the Pacific.

Americans were itching for a final victory to celebrate. They were anxious for the war to end. They desperately wanted the killing to stop. They were confident that the victory would come but worried about how long it would take and fearful of the cost that might need to be paid in the final push.

The readiness of the Allies for victory was witnessed on August 9th with the dropping of the second of the atomic bombs on Nagasaki. False news reports spread throughout the Allied nations that the Japanese had surrendered. Many Americans, Brits, Filipinos, Chinese and others broke into spontaneous celebrations lasting in some instances for several days.

On the evening of August 14, 1945, President Truman finally made the announcement that everyone had been anticipating--the Japanese had accepted the terms of the surrender, thus ending World War II. This time the reports were true. Victory celebrations erupted worldwide.

In the Leyte Gulf, ships of the U.S. Pacific Fleet lit up the sky with a pyrotechnic display worthy of an American Fourth of July. In New York City, streets were already festooned with decoration. Flags were prominently displayed. Tickertape and confetti rained downward. Thousands of jubilant civilians and military personnel flooded Time Square. Upon the flashing of president Truman's announcement of the Japanese surrender, cheers rose from the throng, sirens blew and car horns honked. Eight million people were estimated to have participated in the victory celebrations around New York City. A record 4,863 tons of paper were collected by the New York City Sanitation Department in the space of one day.

In San Francisco, bedlam reigned. The streets were jammed with people. Some swimming in fountains, others dancing in the streets. When the celebration grew destructive, civilian and military law enforcement officials dispersed the unruly crowd.

Despite a cloudburst, crowds gathered in London, England to share in the festivities with the Royal family. The King broadcasted a victorious message to the nation that was simultaneously amplified to a wildly receptive crowd outside the palace. The Royal family made repeated balcony appearances throughout the day and into the evening in greeting their joyous subjects.

In Chunking, China, thousands having endured a long and bitter war against the Japanese, shed their cultural reserve and celebrated in the streets. Melbourne, Australia saw soldiers, sailors and civilians standing shoulder to shoulder in a massive, combined services Victory Parade down Bourke Street. Citizens massed at the Shrine of Remembrance for a special Thanksgiving service on August 16th.

Adding to the chaotic celebrations exploding with the first reports of peace, organized victory observances welcomed back the soldiers of World War II. Supreme Allied Commander General Dwight Eisenhower, Admiral Chester Nimitz, Commander and Chief, Pacific Fleet, General Douglas MacArthur, Commander of the South Pacific, were followed by millions of heroic GIs as they were greeted with victory parades in several U.S. cities.

The exuberance of these victory celebrations reflected the gratitude, relief and sheer joy of the people relieved to be rid of the burdens of war. The sacrifices made by so many had borne the sweet fruit of victory and peace.

The size of these celebrations highlighted the extraordinary impact that the war had made on the lives of millions of people. The scores of people joining in the celebrations showed how many had been directly touched by the war. The casualties of war were always another's loved one. The demands of the war effort involved every American from the homefront to the battlefront.

Over 60 years ago, the words "V for Victory" echoed across the country. These words expressed a hopeful longing and a gritty determination. They embodied these sentiments throughout the war, and today serve as an extraordinary testament to the virtues of valor and service to our country that won the war.

September 2, 1945

The clouds hung low over Tokyo Bay on September 2, 1945. A mist obscured the hundreds of American and British war ships anchored in the shadow of Mount Fuji.

Only several short weeks ago, this scene would have been unthinkable--a war had been waged then. The presence of Allied ships in Tokyo Bay would have been accompanied by the thunder of naval guns. Warplanes would have droned overhead, and the smell of gunpowder and sweat would have presided over scenes of destruction and death.

Yet, on September 2, 1945, the guns were silent--the occasion for battle now over. The Japanese had had enough. Their losses had been staggering. Many of their cities were in ruins--two lay destroyed by atomic weapons. Surrender was the order of the day.

The world's attention was riveted on a particular battleship in Tokyo Bay. The vessel bore the name of the American Commander-in-Chief's home state--the USS Missouri. This imposing weapon of war provided the stage for Japan's surrender. Many dignitaries, crewmen, press and guests would be aboard for the surrender ceremony.

The flag flying on the USS Missouri was the same flag that flew above the U.S. Capitol on December 7, 1941. Displayed aboard the ship was this proud flag bearing thirty-one stars that had escorted Admiral Matthew Perry on his historic mission to Japan in 1853.

The veranda deck of the USS Missouri stood carefully prepared for this ceremony. A requisitioned mess table awaited the surrender documents to be signed upon it. A green baize cloth covered the table. Two chairs were placed on its opposite sides. Microphones were positioned to allow the proceeding to be recorded and broadcast around the world. Two copies of the surrender document--one written in English and the other in Japanese, were prepared for signing.

0730. (Military time)   The military and foreign press were delivered to the USS Missouri by destroyers.

0800.   Fleet Admiral Chester Nimitz arrived by barge from the USS South Dakota. The Admiral's blue five-star flag was hoisted on the Missouri. The Admiral was piped aboard as the "Admiral's March" played.

0830.   Officers and other dignitaries took their assigned places aboard the USS Missouri.

0840.   General of the Army Douglas MacArthur and his aides arrived by destroyer. General MacArthur's red, five-star flag was raised alongside that of Admiral Nimitz's.

0855.   The destroyer USS Landsdowne carried the eleven Japanese envoys to the surrender ceremony. They boarded the battleship without receiving honors and took their assigned places on the veranda deck.

Following the arrival of the Japanese delegation, an invocation was given by the chaplain, followed by the playing of the National Anthem.

S-Hour.   Master of Ceremonies, General MacArthur, orders the Japanese to come forward and sign the Instrument of Surrender. Japanese Foreign Minister Mamoru Shigemitsu prepares to sign the surrender documents.

0904.   Foreign minister Shigemitsu signs the instrument of surrender. Next to sign was General Yoshijori Umezu representing the Imperial Japanese Army.

0925.   General MacArthur concluded the ceremony. As if on cue, the gray mist of Tokyo Bay gave way to bright sunshine. More than one thousand U.S. warplanes including B-29s then swept over Tokyo Bay in a dramatic demonstration of the airpower that had helped win World War II.

On Memorial Day, 2001, I had the privilege to visit the USS Missouri--now a floating museum at Pearl Harbor, Hawaii. I toured the stately ship from bow to stern, climbing up its bridge and walking the decks where history had been made. As I approached the area that the historic signing took place some 55 years ago, I could feel the pride of "Victory" in the accomplishments of our combined forces in having won the war. Visiting this famous ship provided me an unparalleled experience and the inspiration to author this book.

Martin S. Jacobs

About the Author

Born in 1943, **Martin S. Jacobs** grew up surrounded by the reality of war. His mother was a war volunteer and his dad served for Uncle Sam. Even so, Martin credits his love of collecting the prolific "V for Victory" from inspiring war stories from his father, a love for his country and a respect for all veterans. Martin's collection is featured in this book. Other books authored by Martin S. Jacobs are *World War II Homefront Collectibles-Price and Identification Guide"* and co-authored *Remember Pearl Harbor Collectibles*. He is also a major contributor to the collectible books titled *To Win The War* and *For The Boys*. In addition, he has authored 75 articles on WWII Homefront collectibles.

Today, Martin resides in San Francisco with his family. He welcomes letters or e-mail from his readers who would like to share their fond memories from World War II or any interesting collectibles. Martin S. Jacobs can be reached by e-mail: Mjacobs784@aol.com, telephone: (415) 661-7552 or by mail: P.O. Box 22026, San Francisco, CA 94122.

Martin S. Jacobs, age 2, sits on the bumper of his parent's 1943 Chevy Coupe. He became a member of the Lone Ranger Victory Corps in 1945. His first "V" collectible, a Lone Ranger tin-fold tab pin is still a part of his vast collection of over 1,000 "V for Victory" items he cherishes today.

Contributors

Larry & Kay Shedwick of Ford City, PA, are retired high school science teachers who now teach history to interested groups. Over the past 10 years, they have built an extensive collection of homefront memorabilia from "Remember Pearl Harbor" to "V for Victory" items which they enjoy displaying and speaking about. Special thanks to Larry and Kay, for contributing photos from their personal collection for this book. Their e-mail address is: lshomefront@webtv.net.

Jackie Bunge from Orange, CA has collected "V" collectibles for more than four years. As a student at Chapman University, she started dressing in 1940's style and wearing "V" pins daily. She also collects Pearl Harbor items along with pillow cases and military wedding cake toppers. Her e-mail address is: Jacki4268@aol.com.

Contributors, cont.

John D. "Jack" Matthews was born in 1932. His collection of German-made composition figures and tinplate toys has a world-wide reputation as does his collection of WWII military toys and games. The later is the subject of his 1994 book, *Toys Go To War*. Jack and his wife, Meriam, divide their time between South Carolina and their North Carolina mountain home "Viewpoint." Jack's e-mail address is: jmatth@mindspring.com.

Mike Parise of Campbell, OH was born in 1938. He grew up watching people celebrating the end of WWII. As a young boy, Mike collected whatever he could that related to World War II such as PT boats, model airplanes, Victory items and Captain Marvel. Today, Mike and his wife, Jo, are both retired after raising 5 children. He is now a full-time collector and a part-time dealer. His e-mail address is: Mparise874@aol.com.

John Stapanik of Pittsburgh, PA, has been collecting AAF and Homefront items for the past 13 years. Although his collection consists mainly of bullion patches, headgear, goggles, gloves and oxygen masks, he says he is hooked on Homefront items, especially ones containing the famous "V." Today, John is the marketing manager for an insurance company outside of Pittsburgh. He has been married to his wife, Roberta, for 26 years. His e-mail address is: Ramalama@city-net.com.

Frank B. Arian, MD was born in Los Angeles, CA. He is a graduate of University of California at Davis and Case Western University School of Medicine. Besides practicing medicine, he is a devoted collector of Homefront items. He is the co-author of "Remember Pearl Harbor Collectibles" and is the founder of the cyber-museum, www.ww2homefront.com. His e-mail address is Packratdoc@webtv.net.

Bill Retskin of Asheville, NC, has been collecting since he was a child. Since the early 1980's, he has been an avid collector of matchcovers, pocket knives, advertising signs and cast iron miniatures. He has also authored 3 books, *The Matchcover Collector* edition 1 and 2 and *Matchcovers of the 1939 New York World's Fair*. His e-mail address is: bill@matchcovers.com.

Guy Williams of Quincy, IL, has probably the largest collection of Victory banks in the country. He was very generous in contributing photos for this book from his personal collection of over 200 World War II coin banks. His e-mail address is: guy.Williams@bfi.com.

More Collectible Books!

World War II Homefront Collectibles-Identification & Price Guide
By Martin S. Jacobs. Softbound, 8 1/2" x 11," 208 pages, 16 pages of color, 600 black and white illustrations. A 2000 Krause Publication. **$22.95 each** plus $3.95 Priority Mail (CA residents add 8.5% sales tax).

Remember Pearl Harbor Collectibles
By Martin S. Jacobs and Frank Arian, MD. Softbound, 8 1/2" x 11," 88 pages, 17 pages of color, 375 black and white photos with price value insert. A 2001 Pictorial Histories Publication. **$14.95 each** plus $3.50 Priority Mail (CA residents add 8.5% sales tax).

To Win The War
From the collections of Martin S. Jacobs, Gary Slokoff, Jack Matthews, Jim Osborne, Ken Fleck, Merv Bloch and Stan Cohen. Softbound, 8 1/2" x 11," 178 pages with over 800 full color photos. A 1995 Pictorial Histories Publication. **$29.95 each** plus $3.95 Priority Mail (CA residents add 8.5% sales tax).

Make checks or Money Orders to Martin S. Jacobs and mail to: Collectible Books, Dept. 2001 P.O. Box 22026 San Francisco, CA 94122

Newspapers ($35-45)

1778   1943

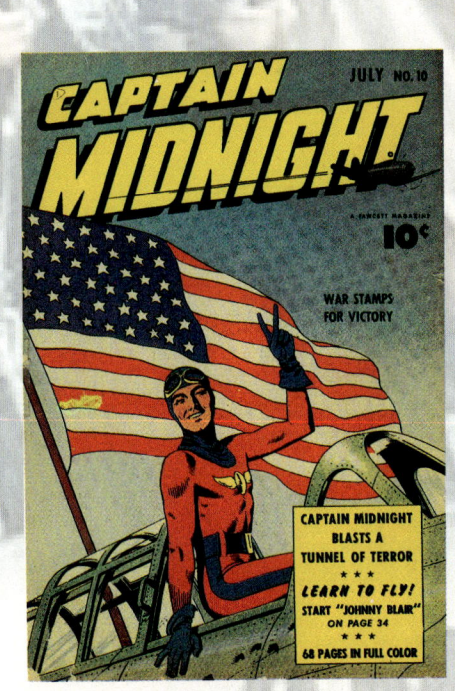

Assorted Comics ($175-225)

AMERICANS
will always fight for liberty

Assorted Posters ($175-225)

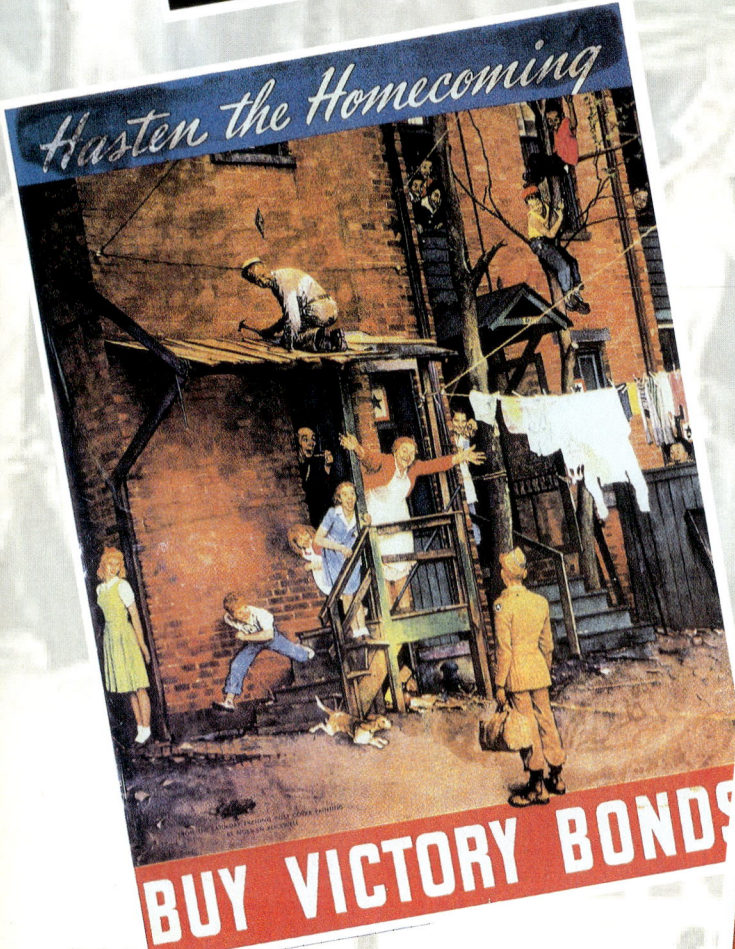

Scorecard ($75-100)

Booklet ($15-20)

Cloth Patch ($15-20)

Board Game ($100-125)

Bakelite Pin ($400-450)

Assorted Stickers ($15-20)

Assorted Greeting Cards ($15-20)

Assorted Music Sheets ($15-20)

Hardcover Book ($100-125)

Bank ($100-125)

Puzzle ($25-35)

Cloth Patch ($20-25)

Sticker ($3-5)

1943

Assorted Postal Covers ($15-20)

Assorted Post Cards ($10-15)

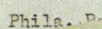

Poster ($125-150)

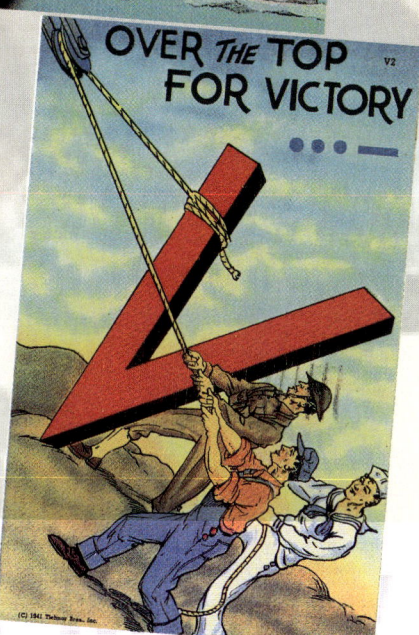

Punch Board ($1,000-1,300)

Puzzle ($30-35)

($55-65)

Toy ($20-25)

Scrapbook ($30-35)

Paint Book ($35-45)

Penny Drop ($500-525)

Match Cover ($4-6)

Cigarettes ($50-75)

Decal ($15-20)

Chalkware ($50-75)

Jeweled Pin ($65-70)

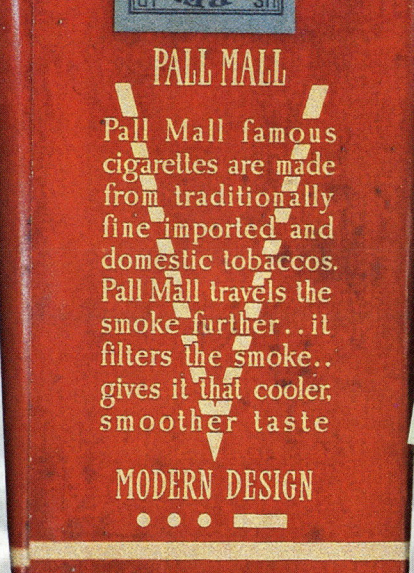

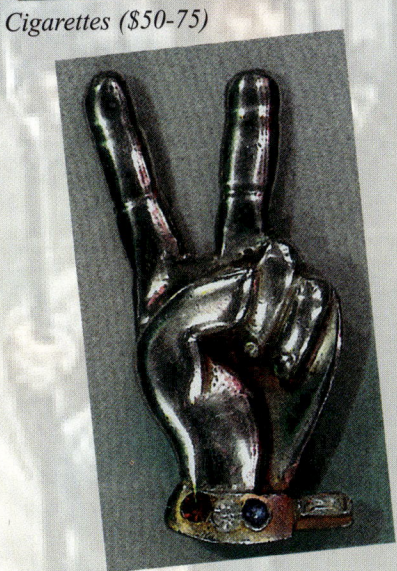

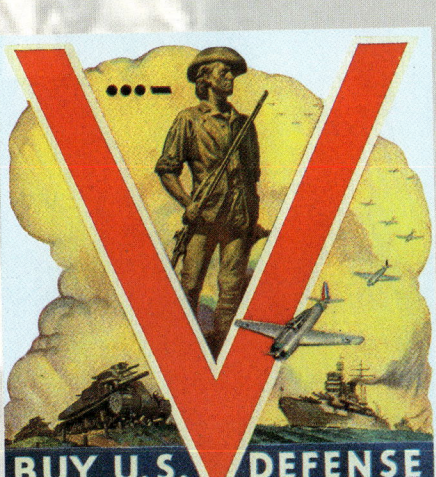

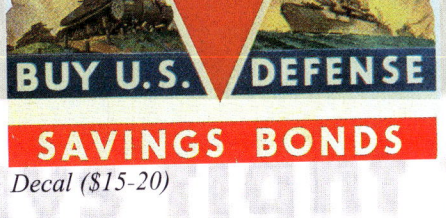

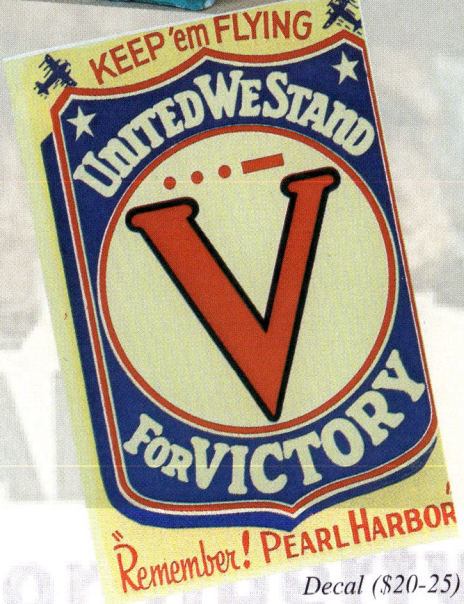

Pot Metal Pin ($45-55)

Sticker ($3-5)

Decal ($15-20)

Decal ($20-25)

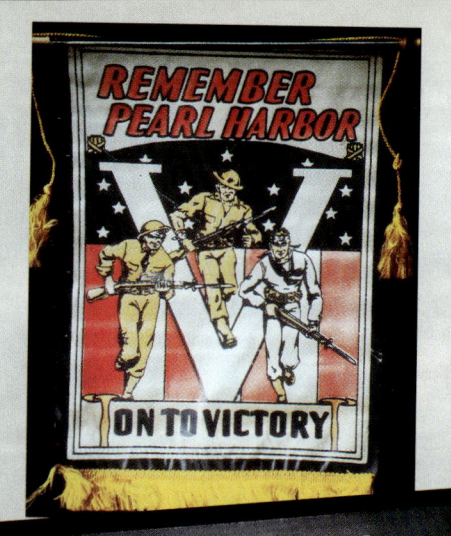

Assorted Silk Banners ($45-55)

License Plate ($45-55)

Assorted Pin-back Buttons ($20-25)

Hard Cover Book ($45-55)

Stand Up ($15-20)